WM420

Learner's Workbook for
Interviewing for Solutions

SECOND EDITION

PETER DE JONG

INSOO KIM BERG

BROOKS/COLE

THOMSON LEARNING

Australia • Canada • Mexico • Singapore • Spain • United Kingdom • United States

BROOKS/COLE

THOMSON LEARNING

Assistant Editor: *Alma Dea Michelena*
Editorial Assistant: *Sheila Walsh*
Production Coordinator: *Dorothy Bell*
Cover Design: *Roy R. Neuhaus*

Cover Photo: *Jake Wyman/Photonica*
Print Buyer: *Micky Lawler*
Printing and Binding: *Globus Printing*

For more information about this or any other Brooks/Cole product, contact:
BROOKS/COLE
511 Forest Lodge Road
Pacific Grove, CA 93950 USA
www.brookscole.com
1-800-423-0563 (Thomson Learning Academic Resource Center)

Printed in the United States of America

10 9 8 7 6 5 4 3 2

ISBN 0-534-58474-8

TABLE OF CONTENTS

Introduction

This workbook is designed to accompany the second edition of our text, *Interviewing for Solutions*. It contains several exercises intended to help you put the skills described in our book into practice with clients. It also contains an appendix of Solution-Building Tools that you can use to complete the exercises and draw on later in your professional practice. The exercises are based on what we have learned from teaching courses and workshops on solution-focused interviewing for several years. They are sequenced to promote optimum learning. Past students and participants in our workshops have told us that they are challenging and fun to do. We hope that you will learn from them and enjoy doing them at the same time.

GOALS OF THE LEARNING ACTIVITIES

- To provide opportunities for practicing the interviewing skills described in *Interviewing for Solutions* and demonstrated on the accompanying videotape.
- To stimulate discussion of issues related to using solution-focused skills in professional practice.

These goals encompass more specific learning objectives. Learning objectives are identified at different points throughout this workbook. They, along with the workbook, are organized according to the chapter layout in *Interviewing for Solutions*.

OUR APPROACH

Believing is seeing.
Doing is knowing.

Those learning a solution-building approach have remarked to us again and again that learning it well requires "a change to a different way of thinking." In Chapters 1 and 2 of our book we call this change a paradigm shift. It is a shift away from seeing ourselves as "problem-solvers" and asking questions of our clients from a mindset which views clients as needing our expert assessments and interventions to viewing ourselves as conversational artists who ask solution-focused questions from a not-knowing posture. This posture views our clients as competent to figure out what it is they want to have different in their lives and how to go about making that happen.

It is easier to understand the theoretical differences between problem solving and solution building than it is to make the shift from problem-focused to solution-focused interviewing. For many, making the shift is like going from doing things right-handed to doing them left-handed. The biggest challenge is to learn how to sustain solution-focused conversations with clients. Most interviewers learn quickly how to ask the miracle question, exception questions, and coping questions; however, they find it more challenging to help clients to amplify their answers. Learners have told us that getting started is not as difficult as figuring out the next solution-focused question. It is easy to get "stuck" and, when that happens, to return to problem-focused questions. Getting stuck is common because clients often respond initially to solution-focused questions with silence or by saying "I don't know," or by giving a problem-focused answer.

Experience has taught us that discovery-based learning is essential to making the shift to this new way of thinking about clients and interviewing. While it is important for you to read about the skills together with case examples of solution-focused conversations, it is equally important to observe solution-focused interviews on the videotape and to practice the skills through exercises. These observations and exercises will stimulate you to ask important questions about clients and the interviewing process, thus taking your learning to a deeper level, one which will make you more confident that you can effectively use solution-focused skills in professional practice.

The contents of this workbook reflect our belief about the need for discovery-based learning. The workbook includes many learning exercises. Some of these are meant to be done in a group setting such as a class or workshop. Others are individual exercises that you can do on your own. The third type are role-play exercises which can be done in a group setting such as a learning laboratory or with a learning partner at your convenience. Each type is described below.

LEARNING ACTIVITIES

Class Exercises
These exercises are designed go along with different chapters in the text and to address the learning objectives of those chapters. Sometimes they illustrate the ideas and skills described in the text; at other times they require you to put the skills into practice. The workbook gives directions for the exercises and includes space for completing each exercise and reminders (headings, questions, etc) for keeping you on track. Questions for post-exercise discussion and space for notes are also included.

We believe that you should read related chapters in the text before you do the exercises. Experience has taught that learners benefit more from them and can make more contributions to the discussions if they have done the reading.

Individual Exercises
These reinforce your reading and the learning gained through the class exercises. You can do these at your convenience. They often involve formulating useful questions and working with the videotape produced to accompany the second edition of our materials. As explained in the preface to the book, the video includes 22 clips from six different interviews. The clips are sequenced according to the presentation of skills and types of solution-building conversation presented in the book. The clips are meant to be viewed after you have read a given section of the text and before you do the role-play exercises. Doing the individual exercises associated with the book and video will best prepare you to do the practice interviewing in the role-play exercises. As you do the role-plays, you can return to the video clips and individual exercises to continue to sharpen your developing skills.

Role-play Exercises
Learners in the past have told us repeatedly that they really learned the skills and became

persuaded of their usefulness by practicing them. They agree that: Doing is knowing and believing is seeing. Consequently, we have included many exercises in this workbook which will give you opportunity to practice each of the skills described in the text. These exercises involve one learner being the interviewer and another playing a client according to a scenario which describes the interview setting, what concerns brought the client in, and what the client wants different in his or her life. These exercises can be done in class (or a workshop) in small groups or outside of class in learning pairs or small groups. If your setting has the facilities, you may be asked to videotape or audiotape the interviews. Your instructor will give you all the details about how these exercises will be done in your class. The workbook provides a skeleton of information for conducting each practice interview and the major questions to discuss in processing them once they are completed.

The primary purpose of these exercises is to give you an opportunity to practice solution-building skills under circumstances which represent a variety of professional situations. Some of the exercises involve interviewing voluntary clients; later exercises focus on interviewing involuntary clients who have been pressured or mandated to see a practitioner. Some focus on interviewing clients who are making progress, are in touch with their strengths, and see possibilities for a more satisfying life; others involve working with clients who seem overwhelmed, weak, and perceive few possibilities. The scenarios also involve several different settings: college or high school counseling center, crisis center, foster care service, hospital, mental health clinic, probation or parole office, senior citizens' center, social service office, and substance abuse recovery service. The exercises have been carefully sequenced so that you can start by practicing a few basic skills and later add others. By the end of the course, you will have many skills that you can use to help clients build solutions to a wide variety of concerns and in many settings.

So, get prepared to be both challenged and have a lot of fun as you practice skills which you can use to help clients build solutions to their difficulties. Clients have so many competencies for envisioning different, more satisfying futures and for transforming their visions into new realities; it is a privilege and joy for us to participate in this exciting and hopeful process!

Chapters 1 & 2
From Problem Solving to Solution Building;
Solution Building: The Basics

LEARNING OBJECTIVES

1. To recognize the difference between problem-solving and solution-building interviewing questions.
2. To recognize the implicit assumptions of problem solving and solution building regarding how best to help clients.
3. To understand the origins of the problem-solving model.
4. To understand the way in which solution-focused interviewing procedures were developed.
5. To understand the stages of solution building and how they differ from those of problem solving.

CLASS EXERCISES

*   **Exercise #1: Assumptions**
    <u>Purpose</u>: To explore the assumptions behind problem-focused and solution-focused questions.

    <u>Directions</u>: Two members of the class read the Rosie dialogues from Chapters 1 & 2. Other members listen carefully to the interviewer's questions and ask themselves:
    > *What assumptions about clients are these questions based on?*
    > *What assumptions about "how to be helpful" stand behind these questions?*
    Class members write down their observations in their workbooks.

    Begin by reading the dialogue in Chapter 1 in which students asked Rosie questions.

    What assumptions about clients are these questions based on?

(continued)

(Exercise #1 continued)

What assumptions about how to be helpful stand behind these questions?

Next, read the dialogue from Chapter 2 in which Cheryl asked Rosie questions.

What assumptions about clients are these questions based on?

What assumptions about how to be helpful stand behind these questions?

Notes from class discussion:

- **Exercise #2: Problem Talk versus Solution Talk**
  <u>Purpose</u>: To explore the differences between problem-focused and solution-focused interviewing. (Source of this exercise is Steve de Shazer, Brief Family Therapy Center, Milwaukee, WI)

  <u>Directions</u>: Class members number off 1, 2, & 3. 1's are clients, 2's interviewers, and 3's observers who pay attention for what is different between the following 2 interactions between the client and interviewer.

  Part 1: <u>Interviewer's task</u>: interview client about a recent problem so you can make an assessment of how serious it is.

  Part 2: <u>Interviewer's task</u>: interview client about something recent that "went well"; get details about *what* "went well" and *how* it happened.

(continued)

(Exercise #2 continued)

Observers' Task: Record what is different between the two interactions.

Notes from class discussion:

INDIVIDUAL EXERCISES

- **Exercise #3: Strengths-focused Interviews**
  <u>Purpose</u>: To begin practicing asking about strengths.

  <u>Directions</u>: Find two people and interview them individually. Ask each about how she or he has solved problems in the past. Get as many details as you can about any inner and outer resources each used to solve or reduce their problems. Write down your findings below.

  <u>Individual # 1</u>:
  <u>Inner Strengths</u>:   <u>Outer Resources</u>:

  <u>Individual # 2</u>:
  <u>Inner Strengths</u>:   <u>Outer Resources</u>:

- **Exercise #4: Interviewing a Classmate for Strengths**
  <u>Purpose</u>: To practice asking about strengths.

  <u>Directions</u>: Pair up with someone else in your class and set a time to meet outside class. Each of you is to ask the other about what he or she has done in the past, or inherited, or learned from books and others, or figured out for himself or herself that will make him or her a good interviewer/practitioner. Each of you should record in your own workbook those potential strengths about yourself that the interviewing uncovers. At the end of the course, you can return to your lists with your partner and talk about what each has kept that he or she brought to the course and what he or she has learned that is new.
  <u>Potential Strengths as an Interviewer</u>:

Chapter 3
Skills for Not Knowing

LEARNING OBJECTIVES

1. To understand the posture of "not knowing."
2. To identify, understand, and begin to practice several basic interviewing skills.
3. To understand how basic interviewing skills are used in solution-focused interviewing.

CLASS EXERCISES

- **Exercise #5: In-class Video Observation**
  <u>Purpose</u>: To observe the interviewing skills that are foundational to the posture of "not knowing."

  <u>Directions</u>: Write down everything you observe the interviewer do that is useful.

What else could the interviewer have done to be even more helpful?

Exercise #6: Rule of Summary

<u>Purpose</u>: To develop the capacity for non-evaluative listening. (Source: Carl Rogers, *On Becoming a Person*, Houghton Mifflin, 1961, pp. 329-337.)

<u>Directions</u>: Find a partner and discuss a controversial subject i.e. something you feel strongly about. Conduct the discussion using the rule of summary. That is, the first person begins and states his or her opinion while the other listens without interrupting or saying anything at all. When the first person finishes, the second must briefly and acceptably summarize the ideas and feelings of the first person before going on and stating his or her own views while the first person listens and then summarizes the second person's ideas and feelings. Carry on a 10 minute discussion strictly following the rule.

Notes from class discussion:

INDIVIDUAL EXERCISES

- ## Exercise #7: Noticing Useful Skills
  <u>Purpose</u>: To pick out and reflect on the skills that are useful in solution building.

  <u>Directions</u>: Read over the dialogue printed below and complete the tasks described after the dialogue.

  In this dialogue, the client is a 19 year old woman whose two children are in foster care and who has left an abusive man.

  Interviewer: Okay. And did I hear you correctly that you got out of that relationship?

  Client: Yes I did.

  Interviewer: Wow! I wonder how you did that.

  Client: It was hard to do but...

  Interviewer: I'm sure that it wasn't easy.

  Client: No it wasn't.

  Interviewer: So how did you do it?

  Client: I just stayed away.

  Interviewer: You just stayed away from him? That's all?

  Client: Uh-huh.

  Interviewer: He didn't want to end the relationship?

  Client: No, and I got a restraining order put on him.

  Interviewer: You did? Was it helpful?

  Client: For a while it was, but he just kept coming back.

  Interviewer: So, he didn't want to break up?

  Client: Right.

  Interviewer: But you knew this was best for you?

  Client: Right. He was threatening me, threatening to kill me and ...

  Interviewer: Wow.

(continued)

17

Client: And every time he sees me he jumped on me.

Interviewer: He jumped on you, right. Even after you broke up?

Client: Right.

Interviewer: So that's when most women sort of become weak and they take him back. How come you didn't?

Client: A couple of times I did because I was scared [of him]. And the more I kept going back to him it got worse and worse. And then he ended up hurting my son.

Interviewer: Oh! Is that what did it?

Client: That's what caused me to get my kids taken.

Interviewer: Right, I see. So, your children have been taken away because of what happened with him.

Client: Right.

Interviewer: So, how...was that helpful to break up with him or was it not helpful to break up with him?

Client: (in a stronger voice) Yeah, it was helpful. Because I feel that another man don't have no right putting his hand on nobody else's child.

Interviewer: Right.

Client: And that child, you know, I feel that if that child didn't do nothing to him he ain't got no business putting his hand on him.

Interviewer: Wow. You are very clear about that?

Client: Yes. He broke my baby's leg!

Interviewer: Uh-huh. Right. But some women, even though he did that, some women either got scared of him or, you know, somehow think that he's gonna change so they would take him back.

Client: No. My kids come first, though.

Interviewer: For you?

Client: Right... My kids come first...

Interviewer: Really?

(continued)

(Exercise #7 continued)

Client: ...and I shouldn't have to keep taking that abuse. And my kids don't have to take it.

Interviewer: How did you know this? That your kids "didn't have to take it" and you shouldn't "have to take it?" How did you know this?

Client: Because if I had stayed with him it would have ended up worse that what it was. Either me or my kids would have been somewhere dead or...

Interviewer: Wow.

Client: It wasn't worth it.

Interviewer: Really? So, I mean, you knew it, you were very clear about this -- that this is not worth it? No man is worth it.

Client: Right, it wasn't. You know it wasn't worth it -- beat up, walking around with black eyes and my kids screaming and hollering, seeing their mother be beat on -- it wasn't worth it.

<u>Your tasks</u>: First, in the space left after each contribution to the dialogue by the interviewer write in the skill or skills that the interviewer's contribution represents. Use the terms for skills identified in Chapter 3 and list as many skills as you can for each contribution.

Next, go back over the interviewer's contributions again, what types of questions does the interviewer tend to use? Why these, do you think?

Which types of questions does the interviewer not use? Why not, do you think?

(continued)

(Exercise #7 continued)

Do you think this was a useful dialogue for the client? If so, what tells you that?

Assuming you think this was a useful dialogue, what did the client do to help make it so?

- **Exercise #8: Getting Details**

<u>Purpose</u>: To practice formulating questions to get details.

<u>Directions</u>: Statements from two different clients are given below. For each statement formulate eight possible follow-up questions which would begin to get details about what the client said. Remember to use "Wh and How questions" and to incorporate the client's key words.

The first client speaks of her struggle with drugs:

And it's like what am I really gonna do? You know, and I think that the first time I realized I had to make a change was when I stopped doing drugs and I was still going to the tavern and around other people and I realized that if I didn't stop doing that I was going to end up back getting high. So once I changed that and stopped going to the tavern and started going back to the Heavy Hitters (treatment program), everything started to change. You know, like they tell you, "it's a process." Everything is not going to happen at once, like I had thought. You know it is not all going to happen at once and I found out it is a lot of pain to change.

My questions:

(continued)

(Exercise #8 continued)

The second client is a foster mother talking about one of her foster children:

Sometimes, like last week, for a while he can be more cooperative, but um, he, likes to play the Ninja stuff, you know that Power Ranger, you know kicking and hitting. He watched that apparently at his mom's a lot and he brought that over here. We don't allow any of that and so just the other day it was on a commercial of a video that I bought, or rented, and as soon as he saw it, started seeing that, I saw him up there. He took, picked up a stick and swung it like this and then he puts a stance where his arms are apart and his legs are apart and his whole body shakes like he was gonna be taking them all on. (laugh) You know, so I think that's very aggressive stuff that he watched and still holds onto a lot of that. He can't have any stick. I had to take the sword away from the Bible Man because as soon has he gets something in his hands, that becomes, he becomes that type of person. So um, even the cape, you know. He's getting better with the cape, but I mean, anytime he wants to watch the Bible Man now I say, "Nope, you're not watching that!" cuz it just starts it all up again.

He can be ... , but it's almost like he's accepting us then when he's not around his parents for a while And like the last time he started calling us mom and dad, not directly to our face, but he'll say like, "Where's Mom?" and, "I'm going with Dad," or something like that. And then the last time he saw his parents he says, "I call my mom 'Mom.' I don't call you 'Mom.'" I said, "That's okay." So it just, there's always the, I think he's betraying his mom if he likes us too much or you know, that's what I feel, that um, he thinks that he's not doing good for his mom if he gets too close to us, I guess. I don't know.

My questions:

- **Exercise #9: Listen, Absorb, and Formulate**
  Purpose: To practice solution-building listening and formulating solution-focused questions.

Directions: A major block to solution-building listening is hearing and thinking about clients' problems when they speak followed by formulating questions which ask for more details about a problem in order to assess the nature and seriousness of the problem. In solution building, instead of absorbing problem information as the client speaks, the interviewer attempts to absorb information related to the building blocks of solutions: who and what are important to clients, what the client might want, details of a miracle picture, exceptions, strengths, and resources. Once absorbed, this information is used to formulate the next question so that, in solution building, we say the next question is formulated from the client's last answer instead of from the interviewer's (expert) frame of reference.

To begin your practice of the type of listening/absorbing/questioning used in solution building, go to Clip 1 of the videotape and play it up to the point where Kristin starts to ask about Melissa's concern (about one and one-half minutes into the clip). At this point start pausing the tape after each response given by Melissa. For each of Melissa's responses, listen carefully to what Melissa says, trying to absorb the implications for who and what are important to her and what she might want. You may want to jot down her key words and phrases as you listen. Based on what you hear, formulate a paraphrase or question which affirms, gets more details, or clarifies who and what are important to her and what she might want. Below write down what you would say, then play what Kristin chose to say and compare your statement or question to it deciding which seems to be more useful in a solution-focused way and why. In parentheses, right after your question, write down your reasoning in two or three sentences. Then proceed to the next contribution of Melissa's. Listen, absorb, and formulate your question. Then listen to Kristin's, make your comparison, and write out your reasoning. Proceed through all of Clip 1 this way--about five exchanges. One last direction. When you choose to paraphrase or compliment, also try to add a solution-focused question after your paraphrase or compliment.

Your responses and questions to Melissa along with statements of comparison:

(continued)

(Exercise #9 continued)

      Your questions and statements of comparison:

Chapter 4
Getting Started: How to Pay Attention to What the Client Wants

LEARNING OBJECTIVES

For learners:
1. To become familiar with the interviewing activities in the beginning stages of the solution-building process.
2. To understand how interviewers explore clients' problems and what clients have tried in order to solve them.
3. To understand how interviewers can help clients make the transition from problem talk to exploring what clients want different in their lives.
4. To understand the types of client/practitioner relationships in solution-building work.
5. To understand alternative ways of responding to clients depending on the type of client/practitioner relationship.
6. To understand that client motivation and cooperation is based on clients and practitioners co-constructing common definitions of problems and solutions.

CLASS EXERCISES

- **Exercise #10: Generating Problem-Free Talk**
  Purpose: To increase the capacity to respond to client complaints in ways that generate problem-free talk. (Source: Peter Dreghorn, Solution-focused-therapy list serve: SFT-L@MAELSTROM.STJOHNS.EDU)

Directions: Learners divide into groups of 5 by number off 1 through 5. 1's are clients, 2's through 4's are interviewers and 5's are observers. 1's talk about a problem, complaining about how miserable it makes life, how no one cares, and how hard he or she has tried with no useful results. 1's are encouraged to exaggerate their complaints and emotions. Interviewers take turns (one response to the client per turn), attempting to reframe the problem talk into its solution building implications, egs. "So you wish things were different between you and ..." "So what's important to you is . . . " "So what you would like to see happen is ..." Observers pay attention for those interviewer statements that are most useful for inviting and stimulating solution talk by the client. Work at this for 15 minutes or until the client agrees on small steps to take forward. Then, the client summarizes the small steps he or she is willing to take and the interaction concludes with each interviewer and the observer taking turns and giving one compliment each to the client.

Record useful reframes for generating solution talk:

Exercise #11: Assumptions About Involuntary Clients

<u>Purpose</u>: To explore the assumptions behind problem-focused and solution-building approaches to working with involuntary clients. (Source: Karen Westbrooks, Department of Educational Leadership, Western Kentucky University)

<u>Directions</u>: Two members of the class read the Beth/social worker and Beth/Insoo dialogues from Chapter 4. Other members listen carefully to the interviewer's questions and ask themselves:

> *What is the interviewer trying to accomplish?*
> *What is Beth's reaction?*

Other class members write down their observations in their workbooks.

What is the social worker trying to accomplish? What is Beth's reaction?

What assumptions does the social worker seem to be making about Beth? Are they useful assumptions?

(continued)

(Exercise #11 continued)
What is Insoo trying to accomplish? What is Beth's reaction?

What assumptions does Insoo seem to be making about Beth? Are they useful?

- **Exercise #12: The Family Heirloom**
  Purpose: To explore what motivates people.

Description: A volunteer from the class plays a prominent member of the community who owns a valuable heirloom worth $250,000. Other members of the class represent worthy agencies in the community in need of funds to carry out their missions. They take turns interviewing the owner of the heirloom attempting to persuade her or him to donate the heirloom to their agency. Members of the class record what interviewers said and asked that influenced the owner of the heirloom to make a donation.

What did the representatives of the agencies ask and do that was useful?

What are the implications for working with clients, including involuntary clients?

INDIVIDUAL EXERCISE

No new exercises. However, one possibility is to find a partner from class and do Exercise # 10 outside of class. The two of you can alternate being the complaining client and the interviewer who reframes the complaints into solution-building talk.

Chapter 5
How to Amplify What Clients Want: The "Miracle Question"

LEARNING OBJECTIVES

<u>For learners</u>:
1. To understand the characteristics of well-formed goals.
2. To increase proficiency in the use of skills for co-constructing well-formed goals in voluntary and involuntary interviewing situations.

CLASS EXERCISES

- **Exercise #13: The Miracle Question**
  <u>Purpose</u>: To introduce a useful question for helping clients amplify what they want different. (Source of this exercise is Clay Graybeal, Professor of Social Work, University of New England, Biddeford, ME)

  <u>Directions</u>: Participants number off in 1's and 2's. 1's are clients who talk about a recent problem. 2's are interviewers with the tasks given below. Between Part 1 and Part 2, your instructor will ask the miracle question.

  Part 1: <u>Interviewer's task</u>: listen and get details about the problem.

(continued)

(Exercise #13 continued)
      Part 2: <u>Interviewer's task</u>: listen and get details about what will be different when
          the miracle happens.

Notes from class discussion:

- **Exercise #14: Presence vs. Absence**
<u>Purpose</u>: To illustrate one of the characteristics of well-formed goals. (Source of
this exercise is Steve de Shazer, Brief Family Therapy Center, Milwaukee, WI)

<u>Directions</u>: A visualization exercise. Your instructor will lead you through this one.

Notes from class discussion:

• **Exercise #15: Connections**

<u>Purpose</u>: To encourage careful listening and staying within the client's frames of reference. To practice key skills in the not-knowing posture including formulating the next question from the client's previous answer. To practice getting a useful answer to the miracle question.

<u>Directions</u>: Participants number off 1 through 5. In each group of 5, 1's are the clients; 2's, 3's, and 4's are the interviewers; and 5's the observers. Clients can role-play a client or talk about something which has been a problem for them in the recent past. Observers pay attention for what questions get asked that are useful. Interviewers take turns asking one question at a time, their questions must be related to the client's previous answer and incorporate the client's key words. Spend about 5-10 minutes working up to the miracle question and 15 to 20 minutes co-constructing the miracle picture. After 25 minutes, the interviewers and the observer each give one compliment to the client.

Interviewers record client's key words/Observers record useful questions:

(continued)

(Exercise #15 continued)
Compliments:

Notes from class discussion:

INDIVIDUAL EXERCISES

- **Exercise #16: Listen, Absorb, and Formulate**
  <u>Purpose</u>: To practice solution-building listening and formulating solution-focused, follow-up questions to the miracle question.

  <u>Directions</u>: This is the same exercise as #9 except that this time use Clip 2 of the videotape where Kristin asks Melissa the miracle question. Play the clip up to the point when Kristin finishes asking Melissa the miracle question noting how carefully and thoroughly she asks the question. Then, as in Exercise #9, begin pausing the tape after each contribution made by Melissa. Absorb what she says remembering that your purpose in listening is to formulate follow-up questions which reflect the characteristics of well-formed goals as discussed in Chapter 5. Write down your question incorporating Melissa's words when possible. Then play Kristin's question and ask yourself whether yours was equally useful in a solution-focused way. In parentheses, after your question, write two or three sentences stating your conclusion about the comparison and giving your reasoning. Then continue on with Melissa's next response. Proceed this way for a minimum of six exchanges. (From time to time, provided there are enough exchanges, you may want to let the tape play for two exchanges before pausing. Do what provides the most useful practice for you.)

  Your questions and statements of comparison:

(continued)

(Exercise #16 continued)
      Your questions and statements of comparison:

Note: the most frustrating and difficult cases to both practitioners and clients are those in which the goals are not clear. If goals are not becoming clear, ask: "How will you know when the problem is solved?" "How do you know that this problem can be solved?" "What do you want to have different?" "What else?" "What else?"

Chapter 6
Exploring for Exceptions:
Building on Client Strengths and Successes

LEARNING OBJECTIVES

For learners:
1. To understand the concepts of random exceptions, deliberate exceptions, and their relationship to clients' strengths and successes.
2. To increase proficiency in the use of skills for punctuating, exploring, and complimenting client exceptions.
3. To understand the nature of scaling questions and their many applications.
4. To increase proficiency in asking scaling questions.
5. To understand the inter-relationships of clients' goals, random and deliberate exceptions, pre-session change, confidence, and motivation in the process of co-constructing solutions (i.e. building toward a "difference that makes a difference" for clients).

CLASS EXERCISES

- **Exercise #17: Amplifying Exceptions and Complimenting**
  Purpose: To practice the co-construction of client successes and strengths. (Source: Evan George, Chris Iveson, & Harvey Ratner, Brief Therapy Practice, London, England)

  Directions: Participants form groups of 4 . Each group forms a circle with the person with the shiniest shoes acting as the client and the person directly opposite as the interviewer. The client thinks of something which was a recent success with another person (a family member, friend, or co-worker). A success here means something you did which you believe was useful or worthwhile. The exercise has several parts and further directions are given with each part.

  Part 1: The interviewers job is to *get details about the success*, that is, what the person did (try lots of questions; there is no way you can damage this client!). The other two persons are observers. Their job is to pay attention for and write down: 1) the strengths and resources of the person presenting the success, and 2) questions that the interviewer asks that are useful. (7 minutes)

  Observers record strengths and resources, and useful questions below:

(continued)

(Exercise #17 continued)

Part 2: : Change interviewers to the person to the left of the first interviewer. The new interviewer gets *details about the useful qualities* of the client; that is, what it is about the client that contributed to the success and what the client did to make it happen. She or he also asks about the *history of these qualities*, that is, how long the client has had them and in what other past successes they have played a role. The two observers continue to record strengths and resources, and useful questions. (7 minutes)

Observers' notes:

Part 3: Change interviewers to the person opposite the second interviewer. The new interviewer asks questions to *amplify any useful quality*. Ask about what it is about this quality that is so helpful. Ask the client to suppose that the quality played a bigger role in his or her life, what difference that would make and with whom. Observers continue paying attention for the same things as before. (7 minutes)

Observers' notes:

(continued)

(Exercise #17 continued)

Part 4: Observers/interviewers talk to each other about the strengths and resources of the person presenting the success that they observed. (4 minutes)

Part 5: Each of the interviewers/observers gives a compliment. The compliment must be genuine in that it is based on information gained through the interview, and it must be unconditional so that the client leaves the exercise "on fire" to do more of the same.

INDIVIDUAL EXERCISE

• **Exercise #18: Listen, Absorb, and Formulate**
Purpose: To practice solution-building listening and formulating solution-focused questions related to moving toward a solution and getting details about exceptions.

Directions: This is the same exercise as #9 and #16 except that this time use Clip 3 of the videotape where Kristin asks Melissa about what it will take to make a part of the miracle happen. Again, pause the tape after each contribution made by Melissa. Absorb what she says that could be useful for making her miracle happen and what is already happening in that direction that is useful (exceptions). Formulate follow-up questions for details and compliment (indirectly as well as directly). After formulating a question, play what Kristin chose to ask and compare your question to hers always thinking about the relative usefulness of the questions. Write your comparison in parentheses following your question just as you did for Exercises #9 and #16. Proceed this way for a minimum of six exchanges. This is a great way to prepare yourself to do your own interviewing.

Your questions to Melissa and statements of comparison:

(continued)

(Exercise #18 continued)
Your questions and statements of comparison:

Chapter 7
Formulating Feedback for Clients

LEARNING OBJECTIVES

For learners:
1.   To understand that the purpose of end-of-session feedback to clients which is enhancing the solutions they are building.
2.   To understand the structural components of feedback to clients.
3.   To understand how information obtained during a solution-building interview is used to form end-of-session feedback, including the bottom line of no task, an observation task, or a behavioral task.
4.   To become familiar with common messages used in end-of-session feedback.
5.   To increase proficiency in forming and delivering feedback to clients.

CLASS EXERCISE

• **Exercise #19: Discussion of Resistance and Client/Practitioner Relationships**
Purpose: To review the thinking which leads to the bottom line in end-of-session feedback to clients.

Directions: A class discussion about the concept of "client resistance." Consider these questions:
Do you think clients resist making needed changes?
Give examples of client resistance.
What causes it?
What can practitioners do about it?
Who is mainly responsible for it?

What is the view of resistance in solution-building work?

Considering Beth's case in Chapter 3, would you say that Beth was resisting the social worker?
What did Insoo do to respond differently?

What are the implications of these dialogues for how to formulate end-of-session feedback for clients?

Notes about client resistance:

INDIVIDUAL EXERCISE

• **Exercise #20: Forming End-of-Session Feedback for Melissa**
<u>Purpose</u>: To practice the skills necessary to develop solution-building feedback for clients.

<u>Directions</u>:   Now that you have worked through Clips 1-3 of the video carefully, use the feedback guidelines printed in Chapter 7 to formulate compliments, bridge, and task for Melissa. Write all three components below just as if you were speaking to her. Also give your reasoning for the feedback using the ideas discussed in Chapter 7. Then compare your reasoning to that of Kristin and Peter's by playing Clip 4. After that compare your feedback to theirs by playing Clip 5. What's different between the two messages, what's the same?

Your feedback for Melissa:

     Compliments:

     Bridge:

     Task:

Your reasoning:

What's different? What's the same?

Chapter 8
Later Sessions: Finding, Amplifying, and Measuring Client Progress

LEARNING OBJECTIVES

For learners:
1. To understand the purpose of all later solution-building sessions with clients.
2. To practice the use of skills indicated by the acronym EARS.
3. To understand how to use solution-building skills to respond to clients who say nothing is better and who have experienced setbacks or relapses.

CLASS EXERCISE

- **Exercise #21: Connections: Practicing EARS**

  Purpose: To encourage careful listening and staying within the client's frames of reference. To practice key skills in the not-knowing posture including formulating the next question from the client's previous answer. To practice getting useful answers in a "what's better?" conversation.

  Directions: Participants number off 1 through 5. In each group of 5, 1's are the clients; 2's, 3's, and 4's are the interviewers; and 5's the observers. Clients can role-play a client or talk about something they have been working on in their own lives; it is okay for clients to have made progress or to have experienced a relapse. Observers pay attention for what questions get asked that are useful. Interviewers take turns asking one question at a time, their questions must be related to the client's previous answer and incorporate the client's key words. Spend 20 minutes co-constructing what is better by doing each component of EARS. After 20 minutes, the interviewers and the observer each give one compliment to the client. (Do not stop and process (discuss) the exercise during the interview; stay with the instructions!)

  Interviewers record client's key words/Observers record useful questions:

(continued)

(Exercise #21 continued)
Compliments:

Notes from class discussion:

INDIVIDUAL EXERCISES

• **Exercise #22: Listen, Absorb, and Formulate : EARS**
<u>Purpose</u>: To practice EARS.

<u>Directions</u>:   By now you know the exercise. This time play Clip 6 pausing after each contribution to the conversation made by Melissa. When absorbing, be thinking EARS and formulate your next question on that basis. Write down your question below. Then play Kristin's next question or response and compare yours to hers. Write out your comparison in parentheses. Proceed for a minimum six exchanges.

Your questions and statements of comparison:

Exercise #23: Listen, Absorb, and Formulate : Scaling Progress
<u>Purpose</u>: To practice scaling progress.

<u>Directions</u>:   This time play Clip 7 pausing after each contribution to the conversation made by Melissa. Listen, absorb what Melissa says and formulate a useful follow-up question for more details about her progress and next steps. Write down your questions and comparisons below.   Proceed for at least six exchanges.

Your questions and statements of comparison:

- **Exercise #24: Forming End-of-Session Feedback for Melissa** (second session)
  Purpose: To practice the skills necessary to develop solution-building feedback for clients.

Directions: Using the guidelines from Chapter 7, formulate compliments, bridge, and task for Melissa based on the information from Kristin's second/later session with Melissa (Clips 6 & 7). Write out the three parts of your message below just as if you were giving the feedback to Melissa and then compare your feedback to Kristin's which is printed in Appendix C of this workbook.

Your feedback for Melissa:

    Compliments:

    Bridge:

    Task:

Chapter 9
Interviewing Involuntary Clients:
Children, Dyads, and Mandated Clients

LEARNING OBJECTIVES

<u>For learners</u>:
1. To understand the application of solution building to clients pressured and/or legally mandated to see a practitioner.
2. To practice using solution-building skills with involuntary clients.

CLASS EXERCISES

*   **Exercise #25: In-class Video Observation**
    <u>Purpose</u>: To observe "what's useful" in getting started with a mandated client

    <u>Directions</u>: Write down everything you observe the interviewer do that is useful.

What else could the interviewer have done to be even more helpful?

- **Exercise #26: Interviewing a Dyad**
  <u>Purpose</u>: To collectively explore what's useful in conjoint interviewing.

  <u>Directions</u>: Class instructor appoints three observers and divides the rest of the class into two groups. One group collectively plays a child and the other a parent in an interview involving a parent and child. The instructor is the interviewer. Class defines the concerns of the parent, attitude of the child about being there, interview setting, and so forth. Instructor records these on the board or overhead. Instructor asks questions and periodically calls a timeout to process how the interview is going for the child and the parent. Observers record what seems to be useful. Proceed this way for 30 minutes. Interviewer and observers meet for 8 minutes to formulate end-of-session feedback for the parent and child.

  Observers record useful questions:

Exercise #27: Responding to "Attitude" and Hostility with the Language of Change

Purpose: To practice what is useful with a client who starts out with an "attitude."

Directions: Participants divide into 6 groups. Each group takes a section of the dialogue printed below which is from a transcript between a foster care worker and a client (Mary) whose 2 children have been removed from her care because of neglect. The responses of the worker have been removed. Each group is to assume that they collectively are the worker and formulate some useful questions based on the ideas and guidelines for interviewing involuntary clients presented in Chapter 9 of the book. After each group formulates its questions, one member of the class can play Mary and a representative of each group can try its questions out on Mary who responds in role. This part of the exercise takes 40 minutes. Next, observers share their observations and the class processes what seems to have been most useful. Be sure to ask the person playing Mary about what made the most difference to her.

USING THE LANGUAGE OF CHANGE

The following is a transcript of a dialogue between a fostercare worker and a client (Mary) whose 2 children have been removed from her care because of neglect. Mary's 12 year-old son had been picked up by the police breaking windows at midnight and when they brought him home Mary was not there. Protective Services removed both her children and placed them in fostercare. In the dialogue, the responses of the worker have been removed *Assuming you were the worker, how might you respond?* Fill in the spaces for the worker with solution-focused responses and questions.

Group 1

W: The court assigned me to come and see you. I tried to call you and couldn't reach you, so I came out to your home. Do you have time to talk now, or do you want me to come back another time?

M: Oh, there's no good time. Come in now. Did you bring any police with you or anything, or any protective service workers?

W: No. No I didn't. Just me. And all I'm here to talk about is what you might care to do with this situation. So, I'm not here representing the police. I'm here as a foster care worker.

M: I've had a million workers already; I've had a million of them. You're just another one. I've had so many social workers. I've played all your games. My kids have been in foster care before. I've played all games. I'm not going to play all those petty little ol' kiss-my-butt games anymore. I've had it. I've just had it.

W: Uh-huh.

(Insert your solution-focused responses and questions)

(continued)

(Exercise #27 continued)

<u>Group 2</u>

M: I don't think there is anything you can do anyway. They always say, "Oh your problem is Ms. Monroe this and it's that." What are you going to do? Do you think that's going to change me? Just sitting here and talking? What can you do? Nobody else has been able to do anything. Do you think you can do something different? I don't think so.

W: Uh-huh.

(Insert solution-focused responses and questions)

<u>Group 3</u>

M: The system has ruined my life. This protective services worker. She came in here and she took my kids away. She took away my livelihood. They say I have to have an apartment. I have to have food. How can I do that? They took away my ADC. I don't have a Medicaid card. I can't get any help with my back. I owe money to the hospital. I can't go back to the doctors because I owe money. I can't, I don't have a Medicaid card. What am I supposed to do? Ruined my life! It just ruined my life. The system always ruins everybody's life.

W: (Insert solution-focused responses and questions)

(continued)

(Exercise #27 continued)

<u>Group 4</u>

M: What I need, I need money. They tell me I have to get a new apartment, but take away my money. Take away my Medicaid. I have back problems and take away my Medicaid. I had one worker once who gave me money. Now that was a good worker. But you're not here to give me money. That's what I need. I need money.

W: (Insert solution-focused responses and questions)

<u>Group 5</u>

M: The system does not help. The system destroys. That's what I teach my kids. Two things I teach them. I teach them that the system does not help; it is out to destroy them ... and, that they need to survive. They need to do whatever they need to do to survive. I'm teaching them to be survivors.

W: (Insert solution-focused responses and questions)

(continued)

(Exercise #27 continued)

<u>Group 6</u>

M: I just kind of go about my business. I eventually get my kids back. They've always come back before. I'll get them back. They're my kids. Oh. Before I played all those games. All those games that they made me play. But, I'm not going to do it anymore. They say that I have a drinking problem, so I got hooked up with this program and I had to pee in this cup all the time. I'm not peeing into anybody's cup anymore. That's over and done with. Uh-uh.

W: Uh-huh. (Insert solution-focused responses and questions)

Observers record useful questions:

Exercise #28: Scaling Your Progress as an Interviewer

<u>Purpose</u>: To reflect on how far you've come and what are the next steps.

<u>Directions</u>: Your instructor will interview you and other members of the class about your progress as interviewers. Suppose that 0 equals where you were at on your interviewing effectiveness when this class began and 10 equals being the most effective interviewer you can ever imagine yourself becoming. Where are you at on that scale at this time? What are you doing in your interviews that tells you that? And so forth. There is space below for you to write your answers.

What number are you at right now? _____

What are you doing in your interviews that tells you that you are at a _____ (number you gave)?

What else tells you are at a _____ ?

Suppose you were one number higher, what would you be doing differently?

(continued)

(Exercise #28 continued)

Suppose you were one number higher, what would your "clients" notice you doing differently?

Suppose you were three numbers higher, what would be happening that would tell you, "Wow, have I improved!!"

What will it take for you to move up one number? What else?

Who could be most helpful to you in moving up one number? What could they do that would be useful to you? What would it take for that to happen?

What could be done differently in this class that would be useful in your efforts to move up the scale?

INDIVIDUAL EXERCISES

• **Exercise #29: Listen, Absorb, and Formulate : Scaling with a Child**
Purpose: To practice interviewing a child.

Directions: Do this exercise using Clip 15. Begin at that point in the clip where Insoo starts asking Sam to scale his progress on controlling his temper at school. Pause after each contribution by Sam and formulate the next question based on what Sam has said so far. Write your questions and comparisons below. Do a minimum of six exchanges.

Your questions and statements of comparison:

- **Exercise #30: Listen, Absorb, and Formulate : Conjoint Interviewing**
Purpose: To practice getting started and beginning formulating goals with a dyad.

Directions: Do this exercise using Clip 13. Begin at that point in the clip where Insoo starts asking Alex and his mother what needs to come out of their meeting for each to say it was helpful. Pause after each contribution by Alex or his mother, formulate the next question, write it down, play Insoo's next question, and make and write down your comparisons. Proceed for at least six exchanges in Clip 13 this way. If you want more individual practice with a dyad, do the same exercise with Clip 14 where Insoo uses scaling to work toward a common goal.

Your questions to Alex and his mother and statements of comparison:

Exercise #31: Listen, Absorb, and Formulate with a Mandated Client

Purpose: To practice getting started with a mandated client, getting the client's understandings, co-constructing competence and cooperation, and getting the client's understandings of the mandating agent's expectations.

Directions: Do this exercise using Clips 8, 9, 10, and 11. These four clips involve the lines of questioning which are especially useful with mandated clients and which you would use consistently right from the beginning with a mandated client; so, they are worth careful practice. When done well, client resistance evaporates and you can move on to the miracle question and scaling. Minimum of six exchanges for each clip.

Your questions to Tim and statements of comparison:

(Exercise #31 continued)

Your questions to Tim and statements of comparison:

- **Exercise #32: Forming End-of-Session Feedback for Alex and his mother, and Tim**
  <u>Purpose</u>: To practice the skills necessary to develop solution-building feedback for clients.

  <u>Directions</u>: Using the guidelines from Chapter 7, formulate compliments, bridge, and task for Alex and his mother (after watching Clips 13 & 14). Write out the three parts of your message below and then compare your feedback to Insoo's which is printed in Appendix C of this workbook. Do the same for Tim after watching Clips 8 through 12; Peter's end-of-session feedback for Tim is printed in Appendix C.

  Your feedback for Alex and Nancy:

  Compliments:

  Bridge:

  Task:

(continued)

(Exercise #32 continued)
Your feedback for Tim:

Compliments:

Bridge:

Task:

Chapter 10
Interviewing in Crisis Situations

LEARNING OBJECTIVES

<u>For learners</u>:
1. To understand that a solution-building approach to crisis cases is a straightforward adaptation of the approach used with all cases.
2. To understand the forms and use of coping questions and scaling questions in such cases.
3. To understand how a solution-building approach incorporates the gathering of problem-assessment information in crisis cases.
4. To increase proficiency in the use of skills indicated by the acronym EARS.
5. To increase proficiency in the use of skills used to respond to clients who experience crises, setbacks, relapses, and no progress.

CLASS EXERCISE

- **Exercise #33: Interviewing a Client in Crisis**
  <u>Purpose</u>: To collectively explore and practice what's useful in crisis interviewing.

  <u>Directions</u>: Class instructor appoints five observers and has the remainder of the group function as interviewer. Either one member of the class (selected and briefed about a crisis role beforehand) or a role-player from outside the class (eg. an actor or former student or colleague) plays a client in crisis. Instructor describes the setting and what is known about the client. Class collectively interviews the client, using the skills and ideas described in Chapter 10. Instructor periodically calls timeouts checking in with the interviewers and client and brainstorming with the interviewers and observers about what else to do that might be useful. This part of exercise takes 30 minutes. Observers and interviewers take 8 minutes to formulate end-of-session feedback for client. One representative of the interviewers gives the feedback. Throughout, the observers pay attention for what was done that is useful. Time should also be left for some final processing of the exercise with observers starting out with their observations, followed by what the interviewers learned, and what was useful from the client's perspective.

  Observers record useful questions:

INDIVIDUAL EXERCISES

• **Exercise #34: Listen, Absorb, and Formulate with a Client in Crisis**
Purpose: To practice interviewing a client in crisis.

Directions: Do this exercise using Clips 18, 19, 20, and 21. These four clips involve the lines of questioning which are useful with a client in crisis. Start the exercise in Clip 18 where Insoo asks Karen what would need to happen today that would make her say that meeting with Insoo was a good idea. Proceed from there pausing after each contribution by Karen, formulate a useful coping, goal formulation, or other solution-focused question. Once you write it down, listen to what Insoo asked and compare it to your own. Write your questions and comparisons below.

Your questions to Karen and statements of comparison:

- **Exercise #35: Forming End-of-Session Feedback for Karen**

  <u>Purpose</u>: To practice the skills necessary to develop solution-building feedback for a crisis client.

  <u>Directions</u>: Using ideas from Chapters 7 and 10, and after viewing Clips 18 through 21, formulate compliments, bridge, and a task for Karen. Write out the three parts of your message below and then compare your feedback to Insoo's which is printed in Appendix C.

  Your feedback for Karen:

    Compliments:

    Bridge:

    Task:

Chapters 11, 12, & 13
Outcomes;
Professional Values and Human Diversity;
Agency, Group, and Community Practice

LEARNING OBJECTIVES

For learners:
1. To become familiar with outcome data about the interviewing procedures used in solution building.
2. To understand how measurements of outcome can be an integral part of the solution-building process.
3. To understand how solution-building with clients enhances meeting the value commitments of the helping professions.
4. To understand how solution-building with clients uniquely meets and enhances the goals of diversity-competent practice.
5. To become familiar with outcome data about the use of solution-building with diverse populations.
6. To understand preliminary ideas about how solution-building practice can be integrated into current procedures in agencies.
7. To become familiar with some initial applications of solution-focused skills to group and community practice.

CLASS EXERCISE

- **Exercise #36: Creating Discourse in the Classroom** (conduct separately for Chapters 11, 12, 13)

Purpose: To address the content in these chapters and reaffirm the competency of learners to take charge of their own learning.

Directions: Learners read content of given chapter in preparation. Instructor will give directions from that point on.

Key points of Chapter 11, Outcomes:

(continued)

(Exercise #36 continued)
   Key points of Chapter 12, Professional Values and Human Diversity:

(continued)

(Exercise #36 continued)
Key points of Chapter 13, Agency, Group, and Community Practice:

Chapter 14
Theoretical Implications

LEARNING OBJECTIVES

For learners:
1. To recognize that client meanings and definitions can and do shift in interaction with others.
2. To understand how the solution-building approach encourages clients to construct meanings which lead to development of solutions.
3. To understand the main tenet of social constructionism, its consistency with a solution-building approach, and its tension with the assumptions of a scientifically-based, problem-solving approach to working with clients.
4. To recognize the effectiveness of solution building as a single approach for a wide range of client problems.
5. To understand that clients' capacity to shift their perceptions and definitions of reality represents perhaps their great strength in building solutions to their problems.

CLASS EXERCISE

- **Exercise #37: Creating Discourse in the Classroom**
  Purpose: To address the content in these chapters and reaffirm the competency of learners to take charge of their own learning.

  Directions: See Exercise 35 for directions.

  Key points of Chapter 14, Theoretical Implications:

INDIVIDUAL EXERCISE

•   **Exercise #38: Shifting Perceptions and Definitions, or; Is Co-construction Real?**
<u>Purpose</u>: To document the reality of shifting perceptions and definitions by clients in solution-building conversations. This is a research exercise.

<u>Directions</u>: Prior to class, the instructor assigns different members of the class to the following cases from the book and videotape: the Williams family, Melissa, Tim, Sam, Alex and Nancy, and Karen. This takes time to do carefully so we suggest one case to one class member. Go over the dialogue and observe for shifts in perception and definition similar to what we did for Ah Yan in Chapter 14 of the book. Shifts may occur in problem definition (as with Ah Yan), in miracle picture, in competencies, in exceptions, or any area of solution building. Record below the area in which the shifts occur (problem, miracle picture, etc) and the key words and phrases which indicate the shift. You are tracing the results of the co-construction process here and remember that a given client can demonstrate shifts in more than one area. Record all areas and shifts for the client assigned to you.

Name of Client Researched: _____

Areas of solution building in which shifts occurred and key words documenting the shifts:

(continued)

(Exercise #38 continued)
Areas of solution building in which shifts occurred and key words documenting the shifts continued:

Putting it All Together

We hope that, by now, it is clear how much emphasis we place on the collaborative nature of interviewing. For too long, the field has viewed "helping interviews" as something professionals *do* to help clients. We believe that such a view is fostered by the language we have used in the field. Historically, we have called ourselves the "helping professions." Obviously, a "helper" implies the existence of a "helpee" or someone who needs help. This language encourages us to believe that we are experts trained to help clients find solutions to their difficulties. It is only a short step from there to viewing ourselves as *doing something to* clients which will make the difference for them.

We have discovered that when we ask our clients not-knowing questions, and then listen very respectfully and carefully to what they tell us without reading between the lines, they somehow emerge having built their own solutions. How does this happen? It is increasingly dawning on us that the answer lies in the process of conversing with clients. For example, a mother says that she is "ready to pull her hair out" because her 15-year-old daughter repeatedly runs away from home. By questioning her in a solution-focused manner and listening to and seeking clarification of her answers, the same mother is able to figure out that her daughter does not run away every time that she is upset. After more questions, especially about the *when* and *how* of those times when the daughter was upset and did not run away, the mother's self perception begins to shift from that of a helpless mother to one who is capable 75 percent of the time. This is the process in which the client and practitioner co-create a different reality about the mother's competence. Equally important, in this process, the practitioner's perception of the mother's competence shifts right along with that of the mother.

In the preface, we wrote that effectively conducting solution-building interviews requires mastering and integrating many procedures. In this section, we include one last individual exercise for putting all the skills together.

INDIVIDUAL EXERCISE

- **Exercise #39: Using the Language of Change**
  Purpose: To draw on all acquired skills to purposively move an interview in a solution-building direction.

  Directions: The following is a transcript of a dialogue between a client and her practitioner. What would you do differently if you were to talk to this client? Fill in the spaces (right after the points at which the original practitioner said "Uh-huh") with solution-building responses and leads which might be helpful in moving the conversation in a solution-building direction.

  C: I wanted to be grown and I was going with the wrong people doing stuff and by the time I was 17, that was the first time I had ever tried cocaine ...

  P: Uh-huh.

  (Possible solution-building responses and leads; space on next page):

73

(Possible solution-building responses and leads):

C: By the time I was 18, I was really doing it but I had to stop because I was pregnant with Dilisha and by the time I had her by 19 or 20 . . . I started experimenting with it again and by the time I was 22 or 23, I was smoking it. So, I had to take an honest look at how long I had actually been doing drugs cause I was in denial about how many times I had been doing drugs because it's been a while and it's time for me to stop.

P: Uh-huh . . .

(Possible solution-building responses and leads):

C: You know it's time for me to stop . . . while I still have a chance to do something.

P: You have a chance to do a lot.

C: Uh-huh, it's like I say, so much has changed and I had a problem with that ... change. I had a fear of it, like you all gotta be crazy. I don't want to stop doing this because if I stop doing this, what am I gonna do?

P: Uh-huh . . .

(Possible solution-building responses and leads):

(continued)

C: And it's like what am I really gonna do? You know, and I think that the first time I realized I had to make a change was when I stopped doing drugs and I was still going to the tavern and around other people and I realized that if I didn't stop doing that I was going to end up back getting high. So once I changed that and stopped going to the tavern and started going back to the Heavy Hitters (treatment program), everything started to change. You know, like they tell you, "it's a process." Everything is not going to happen at once, like I had thought. You know it is not all going to happen at once and I found out it is a lot of pain to change.

P: Right.

      (Possible solution-building responses and leads):

C: You know . . . to let go of stuff . . . to let go of people . . . to let go of things that you used to do. So, it's a process. You find yourself listening and you go back to pick it up.

P: Uh-huh . . .

      (Possible solution-building responses and leads):

(continued)

(Exercise #39 continued)

C: So I understand. I had to learn, I look back now . . . the first time I was in treatment was in
'85. Yeah, in '85.

P: Where was that?

C: St. Anthony's. Well actually, I had started to commit suicide.

P: Really?

C: Yeah, and I spent like 23 days at the County Mental Hospital and they diagnosed me with
a cocaine problem and I was like, I thought they was out of their minds. I was like I didn't
know . . . I didn't know. I didn't have the slightest idea.

P: Really?

C: I didn't have no idea about nothing I was just dumb to everything. I was just doing it. To fit
in and doing it to fit in . . . that created a habit.

P: Uh-huh.

(Possible solution-building responses and leads):

C: You know, a real bad habit.

P: Yeah, I suppose so . . .

C: A real bad habit. So, you know I look at all that stuff.

P: I think you've been through a lot . . .

C: Yeah, I have. And I put people around me through a lot.. You know I had a thing like . . .
don't nobody care about me. I didn't care about myself.

P: Right.

C: And you know I thought I ain't hurting nobody so why everybody be in my business and
worry about what I'm doing? But that wasn't true because there were people who actually
loved me for me and I didn't understand.

(continued)

(Exercise #39 continued)
      P: Yup.

        (Possible solution-building responses and leads):

      C: I thought everybody was against me. I really did . . . and its like now when you make changes in your life you can see the people that care, like you and Sheila.

      P: Yup.

        (Possible solution-building responses and leads):

      C: You know, you can just see.

* * * *

      P: Isn't it amazing how many people are really out there who are just full of love and energy and want to help you . . . and you never see those people 'til you need them?

      C: Aw! that was, that was the killing part about it because I didn't know these kind of people existed.

      P: Uh-huh.

        (Possible solution-building responses and leads):

(continued)

(Exercise #39 continued)

C: I thought that only happened when you were old and you got love because you had so many years of wisdom . . . and they always say "Baby , you know you really don't need to be doing that." That's what old people be saying.

* * * *

(Client talks about admiring women like T who get their GED or college education)

C: And when I started coming around and started seein' women who was in the depth of drug addiction, real deep into drugs, prostitution, and stealing and all that stuff and you see them . . . and they manage to stay off drugs five years and longer, and you see the kind of things that they done accomplished and be like, "Damn, maybe I can do that too!" . . . . but you have to stick with the ones that's doing what you want to do.

P: Look how far you've come in the last year! We are sitting here . . .

C: Year . . . (reports how a year ago she was out on the street, arrested for prostitution, doing anything for drugs, etc). I had a lot of things against me then and to look at it one year latter. . . you are right . . . the positive side one year later . . . I've been clean for five months . . . I have my own apartment, my own telephone . . .

P: (Both client and practitioner are laughing.)

C: I'm getting ready to graduate from the first stage of a day-treatment program, I have learned a lot of things about myself.

P: Great, great, you are doing well.

(Possible solution-building responses and leads):

C: Well, there is one thing I am trying to figure out . . . should I graduate with this class or not?

P: What do you mean by that?

C: (with sigh) I don't know . . . because . . . it's like we gotta write this autobiography.

P: Um-hum.

(continued)

78

C: . . . and its like I haven't wrote my autobiography . . . and it's just like doing a fourth step . . . but I haven't told you about the 12 steps yet, have I . . . .

P: No, but I know about it . . .

C: Yeah, it's like actually writing your autobiography is like starting on the fourth step and it means you gotta get rid of all that old stuff deep inside of you that keeps you sick.

P: Um-hum.

(Possible solution-building responses and leads):

C: . . . and I remember before I had a hard time with my autobiography, it took me six months and I ended up taping it instead of writing it but you get the most effect I guess from writing it . . .

P: Um-hum.

C: . . . cause you actually see the stuff . . . your whole life on paper . . . and you know, just sometimes there are parts of your life that you are not proud of . . . but that's when you got to ask God to forgive you for that part of your life. I mean like I look at my son . . . I can't deal with him. My 16-year old son . . . I love him . . . you know?

P: Uh-huh.

(Possible solution-building responses and leads):

(continued)

(Exercise #39 continued)

(Client goes on to talk about her children and the difficulty with the 16-year old as well as saying she went to a school banquet for him last night, where he got his "letter" to put on the school jacket he got for Christmas.)

P: See how you had to learn how to trust that people change?

C: Yea, you know what? I'm glad you said that . . . that's a key factor . . . I forgot . . . so many times I went into treatment and I could never stay clean for longer than 60 days . . . and my children . . . I thought they were like . . . little children . . . they grew up with me using drugs and stuff and I stopped taking care of them when they were like about 6 or 7 years old . . . that's when I really zoomed in with the drugs and stuff and I didn't have time for them . . .   yeah . . . I'm glad you said that . . . cause so many times they done seen me and I think the worst time is to see your mother go a whole year and a half and you really think things is gonna happen now because, you know, we getting to be with her, she's doing stuff, things is gonna be all right now . . . then to have your mother do an about face and go back . . . I'm glad you said that because that's one subject she bring up a lot . . . you know, Sharon, what is gonna be different this time?

P: Uh-huh.

(Possible solution-building responses and leads):

C: You know that's basically the same question that a lot of counselors ask you . . . What are you gonna do different this time? . . . you know . . . and this time what I see different is that I learned how to stay clean when I stayed in that residential treatment for those 8 months and I managed to stay clean for almost a year and a half . . . I learned to stay clean but I had never dealt with inside issues . . . that I've had as a child . . . you know . . . with my mother and my being molested by my uncles . . . you know it's the secrets that you have . . . the things that you went through life. . . and you never told nobody . . . you have any intentions of going forward in you gotta get rid of those secrets because secrets--those are the things that will take you right back to drugs.

P: Right . . .

(Possible solution-building responses and leads):

(continued)

(Exercise #39 continued)

C: So, I'm dealing with that this time. I'm taking a honest look at myself because I didn't think I had no faults.

P: (Laughs with client)

C: I learned it was a cover up of all the pain . . . being in a lot of pain . . . you don't know how to tell nobody . . . you don't know how to deal with it . . . .

End-of-session feedback:
Compliments:

Bridge:

Task:

Impressions of the Course

INDIVIDUAL EXERCISE

- **Exercise #40: Learners' Impressions About the Course**
  Purpose: For learners to reflect on their impressions of the course.

  Directions: give answers to the questions below. Your instructor may ask you to do this in preparation for a final class discussion or submit your written answers as part of a course evaluation.

  1. *What three useful things stand out about this course?*

  2. *If you were to describe this course to your fellow students, co-workers, or supervisors, what words would you use?*

  3. *What do you find yourself doing differently in other areas of your life, even a little bit, since you have taken this course? What else?*

(continued)

4. *What would your closest friend (family member, partner, best friend, employer, neighbor, parent or child, supervisor, etc.) say that you are doing differently since you have taken this course?*

5. *What do you like about these changes?*

6. *What will you keep doing because it works?*

7. *What do you need to work on to become an even more effective interviewer?*

8. *On a scale where 0 equals least useful course I've had and 10 most useful, where would you rate this course?*

———————

(Exercise 40 continued)

9.   *What makes this course a _____ (number you gave it)? What else?*

10.   *Suppose it were one or two numbers higher, what would be happening that would tell you it was more even useful to you? What else?*

Appendix A
Role-Play Scenarios, and
Goal Formulation and Follow-Up Interviews
Around Personal Concerns

ABOUT ROLE-PLAY EXERCISES

- They are meant to give you practice interviewing.

- Your instructor has the details about the role-play development and will share these with the role-player.

- Begin with scenarios involving voluntary clients, then move on to the others.

- Skills to focus on in role-plays with voluntary clients:
  1. Listen for and get details about who and what are important to the client.

  2. Notice and explore the client's key words (about who and what are important to them).

  3. Paraphrase and summarize frequently.

  4. Compliment client strengths and successes.

  5. End the interview with a paraphrase or summary of what the client seems to want to have different, and offer to meet again to work more on defining those differences.

- Structure of role-plays:
  1. Agency (describes agency setting for the role-play)

  2. Interviewer (gives type of practitioner and, in some instances, role clarification)

  3. Client (gives client characteristics that the interviewer knows)

  4. Role-play development (this is the part the interviewer does not know and is shared with the role-player by the instructor before the role-play)

- Structure of practice sessions (can be done in learning pairs or in lab groups of 5 or 6 learners; the number of role-plays is meant to accommodate lab groups of 5 or 6 persons).

- Guidelines for processing (for giving useful feedback to interviewers after the completion of an interview). The feedback given to the interviewer should:
  1. Be descriptive not evaluative

  2. Be specific not general

  3. Focus mainly on what the interviewer did that was useful. ("Keeps")

  4. Focus secondarily on what else could have been done to be even more helpful. ("Workons")

(continued)

(About Role-Play Exercise continued)

5.   Focus on what the interviewer could have done instead when there are obvious difficulties. ("Workons")

(Appendix B contains several useful solution-building tools: Interviewer Skills Rating Form, Helpful Linguistic Skills, Questions Lead-Ins, Complimenting, and several more. Read them over carefully before using them in interviews and return to them often to refresh your memory; you will find them helpful both in conducting and processing interviews.)

RP #1
Voluntary Client
(female)

Agency: Counseling center at a high school

Interviewer: School counselor

Client: A high school girl who came into the counseling office to ask a
               question. She comes back when the counselor is free.

Interviewer's Tasks:
Listen for who and what are important to the client. (Take note of key words used to
describe these)

Paraphrase/summarize the client's concerns.

Compliment client strengths and successes.

Summarize what the client wants different.

Finish with a final summary and offer to meet again.

(continued)

Processing the Interview:
What did the interviewer do that was useful (to discover who and what are important to the client and what the client might want that is different)?

What else might have been useful?

Voluntary Client
(female or male)

Agency: College counseling center

Interviewer: A counselor

Client: A walk-in client

Interviewer's Tasks:
Listen for who and what are important to the client. (Take note of key words used to describe these)

Paraphrase/summarize the client's concerns.

Compliment client strengths and successes.

Summarize what the client wants different.

Finish with a final summary and offer to meet again.

(continued)

Processing the Interview:
What did the interviewer do that was useful (to discover who and what are important to the client and what the client might want that is different)?

What else might have been useful?

RP #3
Voluntary Client
(male or female)

Agency: A high school

Interviewer: High school counselor

Client: A junior is presently a member of the school basketball team which has just won the league and is now entering tournaments. He (or she) drops in your office "to talk".

<u>Interviewer's Tasks</u>:
Listen for who and what are important to the client. (Take note of key words used to describe these)

Paraphrase/summarize the client's concerns.

Compliment client strengths and successes.

Summarize what the client wants different.

Finish with a final summary and offer to meet again.

(continued)

What did the interviewer do that was useful (to discover who and what are important to the client and what the client might want that is different)?

What else might have been useful?

Voluntary Client
(female)

Agency: A high school

Interviewer: You are a school counselor who has received, in person, three requests from a female student for an appointment. All three appointments have been broken by her. When she comes to your door to request her fourth appointment, you have an hour to spare. You mention the three broken appointments and invite her to come in and talk.

Client: A high-school senior

Interviewer's Tasks:
Listen for who and what are important to the client. (Take note of key words used to describe these)

Paraphrase/summarize the client's concerns.

Compliment client strengths and successes.

Summarize what the client wants different.

Finish with a final summary and offer to meet again.

(continued)

Processing the Interview:

What did the interviewer do that was useful (to discover who and what are important to the client and what the client might want that is different)?

What else might have been useful?

Voluntary Client
(male or female)

Agency: Probate Court

Interviewer: Social worker who works in post-adoption services

Client: 16-year-old boy, adopted at the age of 3 months, is requesting information about his birth parents. Note: social worker may not release identifying information (i.e., name, last known address, telephone numbers, etc.) to a minor. The only way for identifying information to be released (short of a court order in emergency situations) is that the correct paperwork be filed with the state and that the persons involved all be over the age of 18. Social worker is able to share non-identifying information with minors (i.e., medical history, physical profile, circumstances surrounding the birth, reason for release, anything that cannot be used to identify the people involved).

Interviewer's Tasks:
Listen for who and what are important to the client. (Take note of key words used to describe these)

Paraphrase/summarize the client's concerns.

Compliment client strengths and successes.

Summarize what the client wants different.

Finish with a final summary and offer to meet again.

(continued)

<u>Processing the Interview</u>:
What did the interviewer do that was useful (to discover who and what are important to the client and what the client might want that is different)?

What else might have been useful?

RP #6
Voluntary Client
(female)

Agency: Community mental health center

Interviewer: A mental health professional

Client: The client (Mary) is a 40-year-old woman. She is a mother of two children, ages 13 and 15, a wife of a successful businessman and a caregiver to her mother-in-law. Mary reluctantly called the social worker who was referred by a friend. She has scheduled an appointment to see the worker and is 20 minutes early. Mary's children, husband, and mother-in-law are unaware of the appointment.

Interviewer's Tasks:
Listen for who and what are important to the client. (Take note of key words used to describe these)

Paraphrase/summarize the client's concerns.

Compliment client strengths and successes.

Summarize what the client wants different.

Finish with a final summary and offer to meet again.

(continued)

<u>Processing the Interview</u>:
What was useful?

What else might have been useful?

Voluntary Client
(female)

Agency:　　　College counseling center

Interviewer:　A counselor

Client:　　　A college senior named Ruth has called in to say that she needed an appointment immediately to talk about a personal catastrophe that has recently occurred in her life. She is 10 minutes early.

Interviewer's Tasks:
Listen for who and what are important to the client. (Take note of key words used to describe these)

Paraphrase/summarize the client's concerns.

Compliment client strengths and successes.

Summarize what the client wants different.

Finish with a final summary and offer to meet again.

(continued)

<u>Processing the Interview</u>:
What was useful?

What else might have been useful?

RP #8
Voluntary Client
(female)

Agency: A high school

Interviewer: You are a school counselor who has been working in this high school for four years and have established a reputation for being very understanding and helpful to students. You have noticed a female student who has stuck her head in your door several times to say "Hi!" and then gone on her way. Just prior to this interview she lingered momentarily after her "Hi!" and you responded with: "Would you like to come in and talk?" She blushed and nodded her head, "No." But she came back the next day looking very embarrassed and said, "Yes, I do want to talk". You have a 1/2 hour before your next appointment and you invite her in.

Client: A student

<u>Interviewer's Tasks</u>:

Listen for who and what are important to the client. (Take note of key words used to describe these)

Paraphrase/summarize the client's concerns.

Compliment client strengths and successes.

Summarize what the client wants different.

Finish with a final summary and offer to meet again.   (continued)

Processing the Interview:
What was useful?

What else might have been useful?

Voluntary Client
(female)

Agency: A crisis intervention center

Interviewer: A counselor

Client: A 23 year old woman has just found out that her roommate is a lesbian. She drops into the center to talk to someone.

<u>Interviewer's Tasks</u>:
Listen for who and what are important to the client. (Take note of key words used to describe these)

Paraphrase/summarize the client's concerns.

Compliment client strengths and successes.

Summarize what the client wants different.

Finish with a final summary and offer to meet again.

(continued)

What was useful?

What else might have been useful?

Voluntary Client
(male or female)

Agency: Family and children's service agency

Interviewer: Social worker

Client: A man (or woman) who phoned for an appointment, telling the receptionist that he was very worried and needed to talk with somebody. An appointment was offered for next week, but he asked if it could be sooner. The receptionist used one of the emergency times that you had for the next day. Client is 15 minutes late.

<u>Interviewer's Tasks</u>:
Listen for who and what are important to the client. (Take note of key words used to describe these)

Paraphrase/summarize the client's concerns.

Compliment client strengths and successes.

Summarize what the client wants different.

Finish with a final summary and offer to meet again.
(continued)

Processing the Interview:
What was useful?

What else might have been useful?

Voluntary Client
(male or female)

Agency: A family service agency

Interviewer: A social worker

Client: A married person who finds his (or her) spouse's behavior upsetting. This is what he told the receptionist when he telephoned for this appointment, the initial interview. There was a week's lapse of time between the telephone call and this interview. The interviewee is 15 minutes late for the appointment.

Interviewer's Tasks:
Listen for who and what are important to the client. (Take note of key words used to describe these)

Paraphrase/summarize the client's concerns.

Compliment client strengths and successes.

Summarize what the client wants different.

Finish with a final summary and offer to meet again.

(continued)

<u>Processing the Interview</u>:
What was useful?

What else might have been useful?

Agency: High school counseling office

Interviewer: A counselor

Client: A fifteen-year-old girl who filled out a self-referral slip to meet with the
               school counselor. She is an average student whom the counselor has never
               met until today.

Interviewer's Tasks:
Listen for who and what are important to the client. (Take note of key words used to
describe these)

Paraphrase/summarize the client's concerns.

Compliment client strengths and successes.

Summarize what the client wants different.

Finish with a final summary and offer to meet again.

(continued)

<u>Processing the Interview</u>:
What was useful?

What else might have been useful?

PRACTICING AROUND PERSONAL CONCERNS

As you already know from your work with the scenarios involving voluntary clients, the role-play scenarios for practicing different parts of the solution-building process are included in Appendix A. Another way to practice goal-formulation skills that does not use such scenarios is to have learners conduct interviews around personal concerns of other learners. This exercise, once each learner has had the opportunity both to interview and be interviewed, offers the different experiences of asking solution-focused questions and being asked them about something which is real to oneself. Your instructor will explain how to do this exercise; it involves an initial and a follow-up interview. Protocols for these interviews are included in Appendix B. Space for processing notes for up to six interviews of each type is provided given the possibility that you might be practicing with a small group of up to five other learners; if you are working in pairs or with a smaller number of other learners, use only the space necessary.

Goal Formulation Interviews
<u>Goal Formulation #1</u>

What was useful? ("Keeps")

What else might have been useful?

What was useful?

What else might have been useful?

What was useful?

What else might have been useful?

What was useful?

What else might have been useful?

What was useful?

What else might have been useful?

What was useful?

What else might have been useful?

Follow-up Interviews
<u>Follow-up #1</u>

What was useful?

What else might have been useful?

What was useful?

What else might have been useful?

What was useful?

What else might have been useful?

What was useful?

What else might have been useful?

What was useful?

What else might have been useful?

What was useful?

What else might have been useful?

Agency: A community activity center for children during after-school hours

Interviewer: Activity worker

Client: A woman (or man) who comes to pick-up her 11-year-old daughter (Stacy) after work. It's two weeks after a first conversation between these two about Stacy. The mother had mentioned that Stacy has been becoming more "uppity" with a "know it all attitude" which has led to fights between the two of them. The mother said that Stacy is "mouthy and tells me off," yet can also be quite "sweet" and very helpful around the house when they get along. The activity worker confirmed this impression saying Stacy is helpful to other children, especially those younger; however, she can also be "cruel and sharp" at times, especially to children who are less quick and bright than she is. Both had agreed that Stacy was basically a good child who needed a little help and direction in bringing out her good side more. They both agreed to pay more attention to when Stacy's helpful, sweet side was showing and bring that to her attention.

Processing the Interview:
What was useful?

What else might have been useful?

Later Session
(male or female)

Agency: A family services agency

Interviewer: A family services worker

Client: A client who is back for his second visit. Last week the client made it clear
               that he wanted help in handling a partner who is verbally abusive: "No
               matter what I do, my partner always puts me down, saying ugly things
               about me." The interviewee wanted an answer in the first session about
               what he should do--stay or leave the relationship--and the interviewer
               suggested that the interviewee " ... think about what was happening in the
               relationship that he would like to see continue to happen."

<u>Processing the Interview</u>:
What was useful?

What else might have been useful?

Agency: A family services agency

Interviewer: A family services worker

Client: A client who is back for her third visit. She obtained a job two weeks ago as a cashier at one of the stores in a large supermarket chain. Getting a job had been her main goal. She is a 30 year old divorcee who has two children ages 5 and 7 years.

Processing the Interview:
What was useful?

What else might have been useful?

Later Session
(female or male)

Agency: Community mental health center

Interviewer: Mental health professional

Client: A single parent in her (or his) mid-30s back for her third visit. The mother is currently taking medications for depression. She and her 13 year old daughter were referred by a nearby psychiatric hospital after the daughter (Sherry) had attempted suicide by taking an overdose of her mother's medication for her depression. In the first two sessions, the mother and daughter were of a similar mind: the mother had insisted that it was the influence of bad friends that caused Sherry to go downhill and Sherry said she now realized that she would not advance in life if she "hung out with the old gang." Both scaled their confidence high that Sherry had "learned her lesson" and would not repeat the suicide attempt. The family was complimented on their many coping strategies and their commitment to improve their life together. They were asked to "keep track of what each was doing to get along just that much better."

Processing the Interview:
What was useful?

What else might have been useful?

Later Session
(male or female)

Agency: Community hospital with a contract with the Municipal Court to provide
               substance abuse treatment for DWI (Driving While Under the Influence)
               cases

Interviewer: Substance abuse counselor

Client: A client who is back for his (or her) second visit. He had been spotted by
               the highway patrol driving erratically. He was stopped and given a
               breathalyzer which he failed. He was automatically referred for services
               while his case is pending. In the first session he remained in a visiting
               relationship to services insisting that he was not drunk and the test was
               unfair. The counselor had complimented him for keeping the appointment,
               especially because he felt it was unfair.

Processing the Interview:
What was useful?

What else might have been useful?

Agency: A family services agency with an in-home program

Interviewer: A social worker who visits "Dotty's" home for the second time

Client: Dotty is a 28-year-old, single parent with 4 small children, all under 8 years. She has recently separated from her husband of 8 years. They had a long history of domestic violence and her former husband (drug addicted) had forced Dotty into prostitution to support his habit. She has been to jail 3 times for 30 or fewer days over the past 5 years for check forgery and prostitution. Protective Service workers also think she may have used drugs with her husband, but they cannot prove it. Dotty says the 8 years with her husband were not all bad, "there were good times and I loved him." Her former husband served 3 years in prison on drug charges. While in prison, Dotty went to work for her aunt selling real estate. She did well and moved into her current house which she is buying. When her husband came out of prison 6 months ago, they got back together even though her family disapproved and cut off relationship with her saying "he's no good." When he started using drugs again, he started pressuring Dotty for money and physically abusing her. She separated from him and got a restraining order. Protective Services is not persuaded that Dotty will keep her husband away and feels his presence increases the chances that she will return to her former behaviors making the home unfit for the children. The first meeting with the social worker was spent talking about Dotty's history. The worker learned that Dotty's goal is to keep her children. The second meeting takes place 4 days later at the beginning of the next week.

Processing the Interview:

What was useful?

What else might have been useful?

Involuntary Client
(female)

Agency: Family services agency

Interviewer: Counselor

Client: Sixteen-year-old girl who has just been adopted and moved into the home of her seventeen year-old brother who had been adopted two years previously. The adoptive parents have told the girl she must meet with the counselor because of problems she is creating at home.

Processing the Interview:
What was useful?

What else might have been useful?

RP #20
Involuntary Client (female)

Agency: Retirement home

Interviewer: Social worker at the retirement home whose role is to work
with clients and their families as needed.

Client: 92 year old woman. Grandchildren of resident requested that the social
worker meet with their grandmother because she is a regular viewer of
cable TV Home Shopping Network. Not only does she watch the show
regularly, she makes frequent purchases. Of late, there have been several
times where she has overdrawn her checking account. Her charge cards
have also reached their maximum and resident is paying only the minimum
required payment each month, subsequently acquiring a substantial interest
penalty. Also, resident is on the mailing list for a number of charitable
organizations. Each month she saves all their requests for money. When
she receives her Social Security check, she cashes it in total, and receives the
entire amount in $20 bills. She then mails each organization a $20 bill.
Resident's grandchildren are threatening to go to court to be appointed
conservator of her estate.

Processing the Interview:
What was useful?

What else might have been useful?

Involuntary Client
(female or male)

Agency: Mental health agency

Interviewer: Case manager whose role is to work with clients in achieving
              independent living skills.

Client: A thirty-one-year-old female (or male) diagnosed with schizophrenia. She
              has been asked by the case manger to come in for an appointment because
              of the condition of her room in the house she shares. Case manager has
              been told by the client's landlord that if the conditions do not improve, she
              will be evicted. Client arrives twenty minutes late because she overslept.

Processing the Interview:
What was useful?

What else might have been useful?

RP # 22
Mandated Client
(female or male)

Agency: Half-way house for prisoners

Interviewer: Case worker for prisoners living in the half-way house. All of the residents
               are still committed to a state prison but have been placed in the community
               on a trial basis. All must see the worker regularly and fulfill a work
               requirement. The case worker's role is to help the residents stay out of
               prison.

Client: Resident arrived at the house yesterday and is seeing the case worker for
               the first time today. Resident is 23 years old and was committed to prison a
               year ago for possession of narcotics. At that time she (or he) was a resident
               of a large city about 80 miles away from the city where the half-way house
               is located. Resident's parents still live in the large city. Resident's year in
               prison was uneventful, according to the prison record. Resident has a high
               school education and a work history of mostly short-term and part-time
               jobs, none of them requiring much skill. Resident is required to find a job in
               order to stay at the half-way house.

Processing the Interview:
What was useful?

What else might have been useful?

RP #23
Involuntary Client
(male or female)

Agency: Saint Luke's Heartside Clinic (medical clinic for the homeless)

Interviewer: Medical social worker whose role is to address emotional and interpersonal concerns related to clients' medical needs and to share information about community resources.

Client: Twenty-five-year old male (or female) who is a minority person who has never been to this clinic. He was referred by a doctor who volunteers at a neighborhood shelter.

<u>Processing the Interview</u>:
What was useful?

What else might have been useful?

Involuntary Client
(female)

Agency: Retirement village

Interviewer: Case worker whose role is to help client meet their personal,
               interpersonal, and other needs.

Client: 85 year old woman, resident of the retirement village. Resident has lived at
               retirement village for approximately 15 years. She has lived in the least
               restrictive part of the home, having her own room and the freedom to come
               and go as she wishes. Case worker has been asked to visit the resident to
               talk about her being moved to the next restrictive level of care, supportive
               care, because of late the resident has had some problems with being
               incontinent. She has been seen around the village with urine-soaked
               and/or stained clothing. Other residents have noticed this and have
               complained about her odor as well. The retirement village has a policy that
               when people are unable to keep themselves clean, they must move to
               supportive care.

Processing the Interview:
What was useful?

What else might have been useful?

Involuntary Client
(male or female)

Agency: A school

Interviewer: A school psychologist

Client: Daniel, age 13, diagnosed with ADHD has been referred to you because his teacher has been having problems with him lately in class. These difficulties vary from acting out and picking fights to despondency and withdrawal. His (or her) father is a recovering alcoholic of 1 1/2 years and you've heard "through the grapevine" that he may have started drinking again. Reviewing his case history, you find that when his dad was drinking 2 years ago, Daniel was removed from his home by Child Protective Services. He has since returned home.

Processing the Interview:
What was useful?

What else might have been useful?

Mandated Client
(female or male)

Agency: Community mental health agency

Interviewer: Psychologist (expected to stay in contact with the client's probation officer)

Client: Thirty-eight-year old woman (or man) who is court-ordered into counseling because she was apprehended for "driving while under the influence" of alcohol. This is her first offense and she was given counseling and 50 hours of community service as an alternative to jail. She is well-dressed and clearly wealthy.

<u>Processing the Interview</u>:
What was useful?

What else might have been useful?

Mandated Client
(female or male)

Agency: Residential treatment facility for adolescents

Interviewer: Counselor at the facility whose role is to help residents adjust
to the facility and eventually make changes so that they can be
returned to the community.

Client: A 15-year-old girl has just been sent to this residential facility. She ran away
from home for the third time and her parents do not think that they can
handle her anymore. She was planning on living on the street when she ran
away. However, she had been caught shoplifting and now social services
worker is suggesting that she live in a secure residential treatment unit for at
least 6 months. The client also has skipped school many times during the
last year, drinks excessively with friends, and has been very difficult to live
with. This is the initial interview.

Processing the Interview:
What was useful?

What else might have been useful?

Mandated Client
(male)

Agency: Community mental health agency

Interviewer: A mental health professional who works with clients on their personal and interpersonal concerns.

Client: A 25 year old male arrested for beating his wife. A neighbor called the police upon hearing the wife's cries for help. Client fought with police. He was booked for assault and resisting arrest. The wife brought charges against him. The judge put him on probation for a year provided that he get help from the CMH agency. If he does not follow through with treatment, he goes to jail. He has a history of previous assaults but none of them this serious. This information was secured from the judge's office, which called to make an appointment for the client.

Processing the Interview:
What was useful?

What else might have been useful?

Involuntary Client
(female or male)

Agency: Hospice

Interviewer: Social worker

Client: Terminally ill woman (or man), age 23, whose physicians anticipate will live less than 3 months. Role of social worker is to determine any non-medical needs the patient has. Worker has also been informed by the physician that the woman has a long history with the Department of Social Services, having spent most of her adolescence in and out of foster care because of physical and sexual abuse in her biological family. Physician believes that one of the tasks this woman must face before she dies is to come to terms with the abuse she suffered in her family, particularly at the hands of her brothers. He has all but insisted that she see a social worker at hospice. Client is not happy to meet with social worker as "social workers have often made my life more miserable than it needed to be".

Processing the Interview:
What was useful?

What else might have been useful?

Involuntary Client
(female)

Agency: Safe house for battered women (women and dependent children can stay here for up to one month while they make decisions/plans for their lives)

Interviewer: Counselor whose role it is to meets regularly with residents to help them develop goals for their future; client participation in this counseling is required to stay at the safe house.

Client: 32 year old woman admitted to safe house 15 days ago. She came to safe house after being discharged from an acute care hospital where she went after being beaten by her boyfriend. She has lived with him for 4 years. Client was admitted to hospital with a broken jaw, punctured lung, swollen heart, and concussion. She was also cut with a knife in several places, including stomach and genitals. Client was in the hospital for 8 days and then discharged to safe house. Today counselor and client are meeting for the first time.

Processing the Interview:
What was useful?

What else might have been useful?

Dyad
(parent and child)

Agency: Community mental health center

Interviewer: Family counselor

Clients: Mother and adolescent daughter. Daughter is 15 years old and 5 months pregnant. Mother called requesting counseling so that daughter "will make good decisions concerning her pregnancy".

<u>Processing the Interview</u>:
What was useful?

What else might have been useful?

Dyad
(college roommates)

Agency: College counseling center

Interviewer: Counselor

Clients: One roommate calls and requests an appointment for self and roommate.

<u>Processing the Interview</u>:
What was useful?

What else might have been useful?

Dyad
(boyfriend and girlfriend)

Agency: Crisis intervention center

Interviewer: Social worker

Clients: Boyfriend and girlfriend. Boyfriend called and requested appointment because his girlfriend is pregnant. Boyfriend would like social worker to tell his girlfriend all the reasons why she should not have this baby.

Processing the Interview:
What was useful?

What else might have been useful?

Dyad
(adult child and parent)

Agency: Hospice

Interviewer: Counselor

Clients: Son (age 32) and his father (age 64). The mother (age 63) is near death. The son is concerned about his father, who "does not seem to be dealing with all the important issues". The wife has been ill for about 15 years. Her husband has assumed primary responsibility for her care during this time. Although he has done an adequate job of caring for his wife, during the past 4 months when his wife has been "actively dying" it has been more difficult for him to both care for his wife and keep up the home. The son would like the social worker to convince his father about the need for a nursing home placement for mother/wife.

Processing the Interview:
What was useful?

What else might have been useful?

Dyad
(husband and wife)

Agency: Community mental health center

Interviewer: Marital therapist

Clients: Husband and wife, married for 3 years. Husband made appointment because he is concerned about wife's shoplifting behavior.

<u>Processing the Interview</u>:
What was useful?

What else might have been useful?

RP #36
Dyad
(parent and adolescent)

Agency: Family and child services agency

Interviewer: Social worker

Clients: Parent and adolescent. Parent calls and asks to talk to someone. Has
                 concerns about the middle child (age 14). Adolescent is all of a sudden
                 doing behavior that is out of character for him or her (i.e., skipping school,
                 feigning illness, being obnoxious and belligerent, not obeying curfew, etc.).
                 The adolescent's teacher has also called with concerns about the same kinds
                 of behavior at school. This prompted the parent to call the agency.

Processing the Interview:
What was useful?

What else might have been useful?

Dyad

(two adult roommates)

Agency: Housing project for the homeless

Interviewer: Case manager

Clients: Two of the residents, ages 21 and 43. These residents have shared a room in the residence for the past two months and are not getting along. Last evening, a fight broke out between the two, resulting in cuts and bruises for both and the destruction of several pieces of furniture in their room. This kind of behavior is grounds for terminating placement in the residence. Case manager is meeting with the two residents to determine what should happen next.

<u>Processing the Interview</u>:
What was useful?

What else might have been useful?

RP #38
Dyad
(college roommates)

Agency: College counseling center

Interviewer: Counselor

Clients: One roommate calls and requests an appointment for self and roommate.

Processing the Interview:
What was useful?

What else might have been useful?

Dyad
(parent and adolescent)

Agency: Juvenile court

Interviewer: Probation worker

Clients: Parent (age 33) and daughter (age 15). Parent has called, requesting appointment. Parent would like daughter to be declared incorrigible by the courts so that parent would no longer be responsible for this child.

Processing the Interview:
What was useful?

What else might have been useful?

Dyad
(husband and wife)

Agency: Outpatient substance abuse counseling center

Interviewer: Substance abuse counselor

Clients: Husband and wife. Husband made the appointment for his wife who he
            says has a "drinking problem".

<u>Processing the Interview</u>:
What was useful?

What else might have been useful?

Dyad
(parent and child)

Agency: Community mental health center

Interviewer: Family counselor

Clients: Mother (35 years old, divorced) and son (12 years old). The mother called
               the counselor because they were fighting and the son was threatening to
               hurt his mother. The mother says she is an anxious person and her son
               carries an ADHD diagnosis. The mother told the receptionist that she and
               her son both have medication but they don't take it regularly.

<u>Processing the Interview</u>:
What was useful?

What else might have been useful?

Dyad
(parent and adolescent)

Agency: Family services agency

Interviewer: Family counselor

Clients: Mother and teenage son. Mother calls in and says that her 16 year old son
               has come to her with a personal problem that she feels she cannot handle
               alone.

<u>Processing the Interview</u>:
What was useful?

What else might have been useful?

RP #43
Crisis Case
(female or male)

Agency: A family services agency

Interviewer: A family services worker available for emergencies

Client: A female (or male) client who is a step-mother. She asked for an appointment immediately because she says she is about "to lose it and someone will get hurt."

Processing the Interview:
What was useful?

What else might have been useful?

Crisis Case
(female)

Agency: Hospital emergency room

Interviewer: Crisis counselor

Client: An 18-year-old, high school senior who walk in looking for help; she said
               she did not know where else to go to get help. She is disheveled, shaking,
               and very upset, but has no apparent physical injuries. It is midnight.

Processing the Interview:
What was useful?

What else might have been useful?

Crisis Case
(female)

Agency: Community mental health center

Interviewer: Mental health worker

Client: A 47-year-old woman named Dorothy brought in by two family members, Dorothy's brother and sister. She can barely walk and the family members say she is "falling apart" because her 19 year-old daughter who has a small child and is dying of AIDS. They also say that they know of nothing special that precipitated today's crisis.

<u>Processing the Interview</u>:
What was useful?

What else might have been useful?

Crisis Case
(male or female)

Agency: Teen advisory center

Interviewer: Counselor

Client: A 16 year old male (or female) referred by the school counselor because the student has been contemplating suicide. The student had written a letter and it was found by a teacher under a desk. In the note was an apology to the family and friends and list of possessions and who should receive them.

<u>Processing the Interview</u>:
What was useful?

What else might have been useful?

RP #47
Crisis Case
(male or female)

Agency: Community agency serving persons who are chronically mentally ill

Interviewer: Case manager

Client: A 45-year-old, male (or female) client who is currently hospitalized in an acute care hospital for a suicide attempt. Suicide was attempted by a combination of medication overdose, alcohol abuse, and wrist slitting.

Processing the Interview:
What was useful?

What else might have been useful?

Agency: Domestic violence shelter

Interviewer: Counselor

Client: A 28-year-old woman named Sherry who has two children, ages 7 and 4 years. She was admitted into the shelter today. She has several bruises on her shoulders and face.

<u>Processing the Interview</u>:
What was useful?

What else might have been useful?

Appendix B
Solution-Building Tools

INTERVIEWER SKILLS RATING FORM

Student _____   Date_____

SKILLS	Impressive!!	"Keep"	"Workon"
1. Making introductions and giving role clarification			
2. Warmth/ability to put clients at ease			
3. Use of clients' names			
4. Maintaining eye contact			
5. Use of appropriate non-verbals by interviewer			
6. Addressing clients' concerns for confidentiality			
7. Getting details about who and what are important to clients			
8. Use of open questions			
9. Exploring clients' key words (echoing etc.)			
10. Summarizing			
11. Paraphrasing			
12. Use of silence			
13. Connecting (ie. building the next question from client's last answer)			
14. Noticing clients' non-verbals			
15. Use of direct compliments			
16. Use of indirect compliments			
17. Exploring and affirming clients' perceptions			
18. Use of natural empathy			
19. Returning the focus to the client			
20. Remaining open and non-judgmental			
21. Maintaining not-knowing posture/avoiding assumptions			
22. Ability to punctuate clients' desire for something different			
23. Exploring client meanings ("How would that be helpful/different?")			
24. Noticing & amplifying client strengths			
25. Asking the miracle question with pauses and completely			
26. Co-constructing details of the clients' miracle pictures			
27. Asking for presence vs. absence			
28. Use of relationship questions			
29. Tracking what clients want different			
30. Exploring clients' perceptions of what is realistic			
31. Normalizing			

(continued)

SKILLS	Impressive !!	"Keep"	"Workon"
32. Using "suppose" questions			
33. Noticing exceptions			
34. Amplifying exceptions			
35. Use of scaling questions			
36. Use of coping questions			
37. Respectfully exploring pressuring agents' expectations with involuntary clients			
38. Getting clients' understandings with involuntary clients			
39. Respectfully sharing context information with involuntary clients			
40. Affirming clients' perceptions with involuntary clients			
41. Maintaining balance with dyads			
42. Focusing on a common goal with dyads			
43. Clarifying ground rules as necessary with dyads			
44. Starting with positives with children			
45. Getting childrens' perceptions			
46. Giving end-of-session feedback to clients			
47. Staying within the clients' frame of reference			
48. Ability to provide resource information respectfully			
49. Pacing			
50. Overall capacity to listen to the client's perceptions			
51. Overall capacity to co-construct solutions with clients			
52. Ability to give processing feedback to interviewers productively			
53. Ability to receive processing feedback as an interviewer productively			

HELPFUL LINGUISTIC SKILLS

Language is a powerful tool and the way it is used in solution building reflects many years of paying attention for the words and phrases which seem to best promote solution building by clients. With this in mind, we want to point out that the following words and phrases are especially useful. As you study and practice your part as a practitioner in solution-building conversations, return to this guide often and check whether you are making frequent use of these skills.

- **Suppose, (pause) . . .**
  This is a good word to help clients begin to imagine an alternative future to a problematic situation without promising that their preferred future will occur. Since it takes considerable effort for clients to set aside the intrusion of problem-focused thoughts, it is good practice to use pauses to help clients make the transition to thinking about alternatives to problems.

  eg. "Suppose your daughter were respectful of you, (pause) . . . what would she notice you doing differently with her?"

- **Instead**
  It is quite normal for clients to not know what they want when they first meet with a practitioner. The process of sorting this out usually begins by talking about what they do not want. Therefore, be prepared to repeatedly help clients to define what they want by building from what they find troublesome. The word "instead" is very useful.

  eg. "What would you do instead of 'screaming at the kids'?"

- **"When," not "if"**
  "When" encourages a future focus and creates more hope that a different life could happen. "If" retains the future focus, but introduces more doubt.

  eg. "When you smile at him and talk to him in a normal voice, what will be different around your house?"

- **"How come?"**
  This question is less confrontational than "why" and asks: "What were you thinking?"

  eg. "How come you decided to run away from home?"

- **Using silence and responding to "I don't know"**
  The questions we ask clients are difficult and require thought; they often fall silent or say "I don't know." When that happens in your interviews, we suggest:
  - (first) sitting back, looking expectantly at the client, and waiting for an answer,
  - saying: "I am asking you some tough questions" and wait some more,
  - saying: "Suppose you knew the answer" or "If you were to guess, what would you say?"
  - using relationship questions, eg. "What would your teacher say that she sees that tells her that you no longer have this problem?"
  - reviewing how the case came to you; that is, looking at who is the "real client" in this case, that is, the person who wants something different; then proceed to relationship questions built around the "real client": eg. "What do you suppose the judge wants to see different as a result of our talking."

- **Difference questions**
  Clients make changes when they notice something is different in their lives; the difference gives

(continued)

them ideas about what they can do to bring on further changes. Therefore, expect to use the word "different" frequently in your questions.

egs. "What will you notice different about your husband that will let you know that a miracle has happened and his problems related to his drinking are solved?"
"How will you know that it is really different this time?"
"What difference would that make in your relationship with him?"

- **Tentative language**
Tentative language is a consensus building language; it invites and allows space for the listener to offer perceptions and ideas on the topic.

egs. "I wonder what will happen when . . . ." "Could it be that . . ." "Perhaps . . ."
"Is it possible that . . ."

- **So . . .**
A very useful word to employ in order to break in on clients who are "non-stop, problem talkers" who "control" the session with such talk. Once clients have some time to express their difficulties and reactions, use "so" followed by a paraphrase or empathic statement and then move on to solution-focused questions. Solution building depends on purposeful questioning by the practitioner; the use of "so" signals to the client that a topic change is coming and gives the practitioner a device to redirect the conversation in a more useful direction.

eg. "So, I can see that you have been through a lot; (pause) . . . when things start to go better, what will be different?"

- **Wow!!!**
We have been amazed to discover that not all languages, in comparison to English, have the equivalent of this word. Insoo is well known for her frequent use of this word to convey to the client her admiration, curiosity, support, and reinforcement of their successful solutions in interviews. With changes in intonation, emphasis on different words, and various nonverbal cues, a practitioner can convey a great deal to a client. We suggest that you practice many different ways of using this very unique English word.

- **Words or Phrases to Avoid**
  - Why?
    "Why" is often heard as an accusation or challenging word that implies the client made a mistake; it often encourages defensiveness on the part of the client. Do not ask: "Why did you run away?"

  - "You want to _____ , don't you?"
    Such questions reflect the practitioner's frame of reference and thereby minimize the importance of what the client wants different. Do not ask: "You want to get a job don't you?"

  - "Yes, but . . ."
    If you find yourself using this phrase, it is a pretty good indication that you are about to engage in a debate with your client. We often can influence a client's way of thinking, but we cannot win a debate or an argument. If you find yourself saying these words, it is a pretty good clue that you need to do something different. Get in the habit of catching yourself in time and experiment with some other phrase. A good beginning would be asking: "So what has to be different as a result of our meeting today for you to say our time together was worthwhile?" Using one of the "question lead-ins" which follow might also prove useful.

168

QUESTION LEAD-INS

Sometimes the most difficult aspect of trying out a new concept is getting started. This tool lists a few of the lead-ins used in solution-focused questioning.

Make use of Who, What, When, Where, and How. Again, avoid the word "why" because of the negative or hostile tone it can convey.

Lead-in possibilities:
- How will things be different?
- What will you notice about . . .
- Perhaps . . .
- I am not certain, do you suppose . . .
- Suppose . . .
- It seems. . .
- Is it possible . . .
- How do you want your life to be different?
- What will you do instead?
- How did you do that?
- How did you figure out how to do that?
- What else . . .
- What did you notice. . .
- What did your colleagues, supervisors, family, boss notice . . .
- Tell me the reason (instead of why?)
- Did you notice?
- What would it take?
- What would you change?
- What small change would you make?
- So . . . .
- How will you know?
- When things are different . . .
- How would that be helpful?
- What tells you that you are better?
- What is better?
- Tell me about. . .
- How can I be helpful?
- What would be helpful?
- What have you heard?
- Anything else. . .
- How do you know?

COMPLIMENTING

Purpose:	For clients to notice what they do that is good for themselves.
<u>Direct Compliments:</u>	A statement with a positive attribute or a positive reaction to a client's statement.

     Examples: I like the way you dress her; That's good; That's great!; WOW!

     Rule of Thumb: Use such statements sparingly, but use positive reactions frequently; both are better when they reflect the client's values.

<u>Indirect Compliments:</u>   A question that implies something positive.

     Type #1:   When asking questions, use the same words that clients use when they describe a desired outcome.

     Examples: How have you "managed" to make "the household so calm?" What other times have you used your "small mouth?"

     Type #2:   Imply compliments "through" relationships.

     Examples:
- What do you suppose the social worker noticed when you talked to her that lets her know you are making progress with your treatment?
- The principal says all the teachers have noticed some big improvements. What would you guess they've noticed about you?

     Note: Because the worker is not the source of compliments these can be easier for the client to respond to.

     Type #3:   Imply that the client knows he or she is doing what is good for him or her.

     Examples: Instead of saying "that's good," ask, "How did you decide that was good for you?" or "How did you know that would help with your son?" or "How did you figure out that it will work?"

     Rule of Thumb: Type #3 is most effective because the client discovers his own resource.

     Note: Often, clients respond by telling you how they know what is right for them, i.e., what their values are (rather than the worker imposing values). Also, this frequently initiates self-compliments, which follow.

<u>Self Compliments:</u>   A statement made by the client saying they do what is good for themselves.

     Examples:
- I decided to quit using cocaine because I got smart.
- I decided that since I was going to school, anyway, I might as well do some work.

     Rule of Thumb: React to the client statement with curiosity. Self-compliments can be an early sign of progress. Later in treatment, a contact dominated by self-compliments indicates the client is near termination.

(continued)

COMPLIMENTING (continued)

<u>Using Client Reactions</u>:

Reminder:	Your goals are for clients to notice positive changes and not for them to accept compliments.
Acceptance:	Some clients accept compliments easily. Frequently these are the clients who also give compliments which the therapist should appreciate though not necessarily accept, especially if the therapist is being given credit for the client's positive changes.
<u>Downplay/Rejection</u>:	Some clients reject or downplay compliments, saying in effect, that it is "nothing much." In this case, therapists may preface compliments like this, "You may find this hard to believe, but in my experience of working with your kind of situation..."
Rule of Thumb:	Always use your professional intuition and common sense judgement to guide you in your use of compliments.

Sample Dialogue:
Strengths Exploration through Complimenting:

Insoo: And did I hear you correctly that you got out of that (abusive) relationship?

Client: Yes I did.

Insoo: (*indirectly complimenting a possible success*) Wow! I wonder how you did that.

Client: It was hard to do but...

Insoo: (*affirming client's perception*) I'm sure that it wasn't easy. So how did you do it?

Client: I just stayed away.

Insoo: You just stayed away from him? That's all?

Client : Uh huh.

Insoo: He didn't want to end the relationship?

Client: No, and I got a restraining order put on him.

Insoo: You did? Was it helpful?

Client: For a while it was, but he just kept coming back.

Insoo: So, he didn't want to break up? (*trusting client expertise and affirming it*) But you knew this was best for you?

Client: Right. He was threatening me, threatening to kill me and...

(continued)

Strengths Exploration through Complimenting (continued)

Insoo: (*acknowledging the severity of the situation*) Wow.

Client: And every time he sees me he jumped on me.

Insoo: He jumped on you, right. Even after you broke up?

Client: Right.

Insoo: (*indirectly complimenting*) So that's when most women sort of become weak and they take him back. How come you didn't?

Client: A couple of times I did because I was scared [of him]. And the more I kept going back to him it got worse and worse. And then he ended up hurting my son.

Insoo: Oh! Is that what did it?

Client: That's what caused me to get my kids taken.

Insoo: Right, I see. So, your children have been taken away because of what happened with him.

Client: Right.

Insoo: (*asking for the client's definition of the situation*) So, how...was that helpful to break up with him or was it not helpful to break up with him?

Client: (*in a stronger voice*) Yeah, it was helpful. Because I feel that another man don't have no right putting his hand on nobody else's child.

Insoo: (*respecting and affirming the client's definition*) Right. Wow! You are very clear about that?

Client: Yes. He broke my baby's leg!

Insoo: (*complimenting strengths*) Uh huh. Right. But some women, even though he did that, some women either got scared of him or, you know, somehow think that he's gonna change so they would take him back.

Client: No. My kids come first, though.

Insoo: For you?

Client: Right... My kids come first... It wasn't worth it.

Insoo: Really? (*genuinely impressed and complimenting*) Wow, you are very clear about this, "it wasn't worth it ...."   So, I'm amazed by this. (*continuing to foster the construction of a sense of competence*) How did you do this? I mean he was threatening you ...

Client: I just stayed away from him, you know. I was scared of him but, you know, my father always told me 'be strong' and that's what I did....

(Berg & De Jong, 1996, pp. 379-380)

GOAL-FORMULATION PROTOCOL

ROLE CLARIFICATION

(Working with a team; team may interrupt with a question; break then feedback)

PROBLEM DESCRIPTION

How can I help?

How is this a problem for you? (Get problem description; if more than one, which is most important to work on first?)

What have you tried? (Was it helpful?)

GOAL FORMULATION

What would have to be different as a result of our meeting today for you to say that our talking was worthwhile?

Miracle Question (Once asked, focus on *what will be different* when the miracle happens.)

Regarding client: What will you notice that's different? (What will be the first thing that you notice? What else?)

Regarding significant others: Who else will notice when the miracle happens?

What will s/he notice that is different about you? What else?

When s/he notices that, what will s/he do differently? What else?

When s/he does that, what will be different for you?

(continued)

MOVING TOWARD A SOLUTION (Use when client can answer the miracle question.)

Suppose you were to pretend that the miracle happened, what would be the first small thing you would do?

How might that be helpful?

Or: What's it going to take for a part of the miracle to happen?

Is that something which could happen? If so, what makes you think so?

ENDING

1. If the client is concrete and detailed in their answer to the miracle question, give compliments and suggest: "In the next week, pick one day and pretend that the miracle has happened and look for what difference it makes."

2. If the client is *not* concrete and detailed in their answer to the miracle question, give compliments and suggest: "Think about what's happening in your life that tells you that this problem can be solved. And I'll do some thinking too."

(If a second session is a possibility, you can ask the client to meet with you again to continue working on the problem.)

QUESTIONS FOR DEVELOPING WELL-FORMED GOALS

To the interviewer: When using these questions remember that you most want to explore for the client's perception of what will be different when either the miracle happens or the problem is solved. Remember too that developing well-formed goals is hard work for clients. Be patient and persistent in asking the interviewing questions.

THE MIRACLE QUESTION

Suppose that, while you are sleeping tonight, a miracle happens. The miracle is that the problem which brought you here today is solved. Only you don't know that it is solved because you are asleep. What difference will you notice tomorrow morning that will tell you that a miracle has happened? What else will you notice?

AMPLIFYING AROUND THE CHARACTERISTICS OF WELL-FORMED GOALS

Small
Wow! That sounds like a big miracle. What is the first small thing you would notice that would tell you that things were different?

What else would tell you that things were better?

Concrete, Behavioral, Specific
You say that the miracle is that you'd feel better. When you feel better, what might others notice different about you that would tell them that you feel better?

What might you do different when you feel better? What else?

Start of Something Different/Better
You say that the miracle is that you'd weigh 50 pounds less. OK, what will be different in your life when you lose that first pound? What else?

Presence of Something Different/Better
You say that, when the miracle happens, you'll fight less with the kids. What will you be doing *instead*?

AMPLIFYING AROUND PERCEPTIONS OF SIGNIFICANT OTHERS

When the miracle happens, what differences will your husband (children, co-workers, teachers, friends, etc.) notice around your house? What differences will your husband notice about you? What else will they notice that's different?

AMPLIFYING AROUND THE CLIENT'S SYSTEM OF RELATIONSHIPS

When your husband (children, co-workers, teachers, friends, etc.) notice _____ (the difference that the client mentions in answering the previous question), what will your husband do differently? What else? And when he does that, what will you do? How will things be different around your house?

(continued)

QUESTIONS FOR DEVELOPING WELL-FORMED GOALS (continued)

TIPS

If clients say "I don't know," say:
Suppose you did know, what would you say?

Or, go to relationship questions, for example: Suppose I were to ask your husband (children, etc.), what would he (they) say?

If clients struggle with the questions or say they are tough, agree with them and say:
I'm asking you some tough questions; take your time.

If clients cannot work with the miracle question, work with questions phrased along the lines of "when the problem is solved."

When clients get unrealistic ("I'd win the lottery!"), just agree with them by saying:
That would be nice wouldn't it.

If they persist, ask: What do you think the chances are of that happening?

Or, ask: What tells you that _____ could happen in your life?

When clients give you a concrete piece of the miracle picture or potential solution (for example, "When the miracle happens, I guess I'd be taking more walks"), take it one more step by asking:

What's different for you when you take more walks?

Part of respecting the client's perceptions is to respect the words that they use for their perceptions and adopt them in your interviewing questions. Thus, the preceding question picks up on the client's reference to taking more walks.
VERY IMPORTANT: If, despite your best efforts, clients are unable to work with the miracle question or define how things will be different when the problem is solved, ask:

How do you know this problem can be solved?

GOAL FORMULATION IN LATER SESSIONS

Work from the scaling question about progress:

On a scale of 0 to 10, where 0 is where you were at when we began working together, and 10 means that the problem is solved (or the miracle happens), where are you at today?

OK, so you're at a 5. What is happening in your life that tells you that you are a 5?

So when you move up just a bit, say from 5 to 6, what will be different in your life that will tell you that you are a 6? What else? What will be different when you move on to a 7?

Thereafter, amplify just as you would for the miracle question, for example, around significant others. For example, when you move up to a 6, what will your co-workers notice that will tell them that you are doing just that much better? What else?

EXPLORING FOR PROGRESS/EXCEPTIONS

What's better?   Are there any times (or days) when things go better?

If yes, when are those times? What is different about them that tells you things are going better? Where do they happen? Who's involved?

And, how do those times happen? What do you do differently to make them happen? What else? If I were to ask _____ (others involved in the better time) who does what to make it happen, what would they say?

If nothing is better, how are you *coping*? How are you making it with things not getting better? How come things are not worse, that is, what are you doing so that things don't get worse?

SCALING PROGRESS (or COPING)

If 10 means that the problem is solved, and 0 means as bad as this problem has ever been, where would you say things are at right now?

(If the number the client gives makes sense, acknowledge that; if not, ask: what tells you that things are at a __.)

(continued)

ONGOING GOAL FORMULATION

Suppose things moved up one number, what would be different that would tell you that things are just that much better?

What would _____ (a significant other) notice different about you that would tell her or him that things were just that much better? What else?

What would it take for that to happen?

How about if things were two or three numbers higher, what would be different that would tell you that things were that much better? What else? What would it take for those things to happen? What else?

ENDING

Summarize what the client is doing that is useful. Compliment the client for strengths and successes. Suggest that the client continue to do what works and pay attention to what else s/he may be doing that is useful but s/he may not yet have noticed.

FINDING THE BOTTOM LINE

Is there a well-formed goal? What is it?

Are there exceptions? What are they?

If yes, are they deliberate or random?

What is the client's relationship to services? (visitor-, complainant-, or customer-type?)

THE FEEDBACK

Compliments

Bridging Statement

Task

COMMON MESSAGES
(END-OF-SESSION FEEDBACK)

VISITOR-TYPE RELATIONSHIP

Here's an example of a message to a client sent for services by his probation officer (from Berg and Miller, 1992, p. 99):

> Curtis, we are very impressed that you are here today even though this is not your idea. You certainly had the option of taking the easy way out by not coming. . . . It has not been easy for you to be here today; having to give up your personal time, talking about things you really don't want to talk about, having to take the bus, and so on. . . .

> I realize that you are an independent minded person who does not want to be told what to do and I agree with you that you should be left alone. But you also realize that doing what you are told will help you get these people out of your life and you will be left alone sooner. Therefore, I would like to meet with you again to figure out further what will be good for you to do. So let's meet next week at the same time.

COMPLAINANT-TYPE RELATIONSHIP

1. **Client cannot identify exceptions and does not have a goal**

    > Pay attention to what's happening in your life that tells you that this problem can be solved.

    Or, since the client does not have well-formed goals, use the formula first-session task (de Shazer, 1985, p. 137):

    > Between now and next time we meet, we (I) would like you to observe, so that you can describe to us (me) next time, what happens in your (pick one: family, life, marriage, relationship) that you want to continue to have happen.

2. **Client can identify exceptions**

    > Between now and the next time we meet, pay attention to those times which are better, especially what is different about them and how they happen--that is, who does what to make them happen. Next time I'd like you to describe them to me in detail.

    Or, a variation of the same observation task when the client says that the exceptions are due to someone else doing something different:

    > Alice, pay attention for those times when your boss is more reasonable and open. Besides paying attention to what's different about those times, pay attention to what he might notice you doing that helps him to be more polite, reasonable, and open toward you. Keep track of those things and come back and tell me what's better.

    A final variation adds the element of prediction:

    > Alice I agree with you; there clearly seem to be days when your boss is more reasonable and open and days when he is not. So, between now and the next time that we meet, I suggest the

(continued)

following: Each night before you go to bed, predict whether or not tomorrow will be a day when he acts more reasonable and open and polite to you. Then, at the end of the day before you make your prediction for the next day, think about whether or not your prediction for that day came true. Account for any differences between your prediction and the way the day went and keep track of your observations so that you can come back and tell me about them. (de Shazer, 1988, pp. 179-183)

CUSTOMER-TYPE RELATIONSHIP

1. **Client has a clear miracle picture but cannot identify exceptions**

   Between now and the next time we meet, pick one day and pretend the miracle. Go ahead and live that day as if the miracle has happened--just like you described it to me. Then come back next time and tell me what's better.

2. **Client seems highly motivated but does not have well-formed goals and cannot identify exceptions**

   We are so impressed with how hard you have worked on _____ (the client's complaint) and with how clearly you can describe to us the things you have tried so far to make things better. We can see why you would be discouraged and frustrated right now. We also agree with you that this is a "very stubborn" (client's words) problem.

   Because this is such a "stubborn" problem, we suggest that, between now and next time we meet, when _____ (the client's complaint) happens, that you *do something different*---no matter how strange or weird or off-the-wall what you do might seem. The only important thing is that whatever you decide to do, you need to do something different. (de Shazer, 1985, p. 123)

3. **Client has well-formed goals and deliberate exceptions of his or her own doing**

   Ralph, I am impressed with you in several ways: First, how much you want to make things go better between you and your children. Second, that there are already several better times happening like _____ (give examples). And third, that you can describe to me so clearly and in such detail what you do to do your part in making those times happen, things like ____ (give examples). With all that you are doing, I can see why you say things are at a 5 already.

   I agree that these are the things to do to have the kind of relationship with your children that you want to have. So, between now and when we meet again, I suggest that you continue to do what works. Also, pay attention to what else you might be doing--but haven't noticed yet--that makes things better, and come back and tell me about them.

OTHER USEFUL MESSAGES

When a client complains of a compulsion

Pay attention for those times when you overcome the urge to (overeat, drink, hit your child, use pornography, get panicky, etc.). Pay attention for what's different about those times, especially what it is that you do to overcome the urge to _____ . (de Shazer, 1985, p. 132)

(continued)

When there are competing views of a solution. There are two possible situations here. In the first, individuals have different views, for example, if parents disagree about how to handle a child who steals, you might say:

> We are impressed by how much both of you want to help your son "not to steal." The team is also impressed by what different ideas the two of you have about how to help your child through this difficult time. We can see that you were brought-up in different families and learned different ways to do things (the parents had said they could see their different family backgrounds at work in their conflicting views).
>
> The team is split on which way to go--one-half feels like you ought to go with John's ideas and the other half feels like Mary's might work best. Therefore, we suggest that each morning, right after you get up, you flip a coin. Heads means that Mary is in charge and you do things her way with Billy while John stays in the background. Tails means John is in charge that day. And also--on those days when each of you is not busy being in charge--pay careful attention to what the other does with Billy that is useful or makes a difference so that you can report it to us when we meet again.

In the second, an individual is aware of more than one option and cannot decide which is best; for example, if a client is struggling with the decision whether to leave her boyfriend, Bill, you might say:

> I am unsure about whether it would be best for you to "stay with Bill or leave him and begin a new life" (her words). I agree that this is a tough decision and figuring it out is going to take more hard work. As you continue to work on it, I suggest that each night before you go to bed, you flip a coin. If it comes up heads, live the next day as much as possible as though Bill is no longer a part of your life. Don't contact him and start to take the first steps toward the things you said you would do differently if you were on your own, such as spending more time with you friends and family and so forth. If it comes up tails, live the next day as though he is still a part of your life--all those things you described to me about what that means for you. Then, as you do these things, keep paying attention to what's happening that tells you that you are becoming more clear about whether to leave him or stay in the relationship. Remember, though, that usually a person cannot be 100% sure. And then come back and tell me what's better.

PROTOCOL FOR FIRST SESSIONS

Client Name(s):_____   Date: _____

Complaint/History: (How can I help? What tells you that ____ is a problem? What have you tried? Was it helpful?)

Goal Formulation: (What do you want different as a result of coming here? Dialogue around the miracle question.)

Exceptions: (Are there times when the problem does not happen or is less serious? When? How does that happen? Are there times that are a little like the miracle picture you describe?)

Scaling:

Pre-session change:

Willingness to work:

Confidence:

(continued)

Compliments:

Bridge:

Task/Suggestions:

Next Time:

PROTOCOL FOR LATER SESSIONS

Name: _____   **Date:** _____

What's better?

   Elicit: (What's happening that's better?)

   Amplify: (How does that happen? What do you do to make that happen? Is that new for you? Now that you are doing _____ , what do you notice different between you and _____ (significant other)? What's different at your house?)

   Reinforce/Compliment: (Not everyone could have said or done _____. So you're the kind of person who is/does/believes_____?)

   Start Again: (What else is better?)

Doing More: (What will it take to do _____ again? To do it more often?)

If nothing is better: (How are you coping? How do you make it? How come things aren't even worse?)

Scaling Progress:

   Current level:

   Next level(s): [When you move from ____ (number for current level) to ____ (one number up the scale), what will be different? Who will be first to notice? When s/he notices, what will s/he do differently? What would it take to pretend a ___ (one number up the scale) has happened?)]

   Termination: (How will you know when it's time to stop seeing me? What will be different?)

(continued)

189

Compliments:

Bridge:

Task/Suggestions:

Next time:

EXCEPTION-FINDING QUESTIONS

To the interviewer: When exploring for exceptions be aware that such questions can be phrased to ask for the client's perceptions of exceptions (individual questions) and the client's perception of what significant others might notice (relationship questions). Examples of each are included below.

EXCEPTIONS RELATED TO THE MIRACLE

1. Elicit

So when the miracle happens, you and your husband will be talking more about what your day was like and hugging more. Are there times already which are like that miracle--even a little bit?

If your husband was here and I were to ask him the same question, what do you think he would say?

2. Amplify

When was the last time you and your husband talked more and hugged more? Tell me more about that time. What was it like? What did you talk about? What did you say? What did he say? When he said that, what did you do? What did he do then? How was that for you? What else was different about that time?

If he were here, what else might he say about that time?

3. Reinforce

Non-verbally: Lean forward, raise eyebrows, take notes. (Do what you naturally do when someone tells you something important.)

Verbally: Show interest. (Was this new for you and him? Did it surprise you that this happened?) And compliment. (Seems like that might have been difficult for you to do, given everything that's happened in the relationship. Was it difficult?)

4. Explore how the exception happened

What do you suppose you did to make that happen?

If your husband were here and I asked him, what do you suppose he would say you did that helped him to tell you more about his day?

Use compliments: Where did you get the idea to do it that way? That seems to make a lot of sense. Have you always been able to come up with ideas about what to do in difficult situations like this?

5. Project exceptions into the future

On a scale of 1 to 10, where 1 means no chance and 10 means every chance, what are the chances that a time like that (the exception) will happen again in the next week (month, sometime in the future)? What will it take for that to happen?

(continued)

What will it take for that to happen more often in the future?
Who has to do what to make that happen again?
What is the most important thing for you to remember to do to make sure that_____ (the exception) has the best chance of happening again? What's the next most important thing to remember?

What do you think your husband would say the chances are that this (the exception) will happen again? What would he say you could do to increase the chances of that happening? Suppose you decided to do that, what do you think he would do? Suppose he did that, how would things be different for you... around your house... in your relationship with him?

EXCEPTIONS RELATED TO THE PROBLEM

If the client cannot define a miracle and relates to you only in terms of problem talk, phrase your questions in terms of the *problem* instead of the miracle. Example:

Can you think of a time in the past day (week, month, year) when you and your husband fought less or not at all?

Then proceed with the five steps given for exceptions related to the miracle.

WHAT'S BETTER?

You can begin all later sessions with this exception-exploration question. Be sure to follow all five steps given above and to use both individual and relationship questions.

Always ask "What else is better?" after you finish exploring an exception.

COPING QUESTIONS

In rare cases, the client cannot identify any exceptions and seems overwhelmed. You can ask coping questions to uncover what the client is doing to make it in such difficult circumstances:

I'm amazed. With all that's been happening, I don't know how you make it? How do you do it? How do you get from one minute to the next?

If a client describes a longstanding depression and one discouraging event after another, you might say:

I can see that you have many reasons to feel depressed; there have been so many things that haven't worked out the way you wished. I'm wondering how you have managed to keep going? How have you been able to get up each morning and face another day?

If the client says she has to keep going for her kids, you might say:

Is that how you do it? You think about your kids and how much they need you? You must care a lot about them. Tell me more about what you do to take care of them.

PROTOCOL FOR INTERVIEWING INVOLUNTARY CLIENTS

ROLE CLARIFICATION
(Introduce yourself, describe your role briefly, describe structure of session: taking a break etc.)

PROBLEM DESCRIPTION AND ATTEMPTS AT SOLUTION (Throughout, pay attention for clues about what the client might want, and what s/he might be able and willing to do.)

What is your understanding of why we are talking today? (Be prepared to share what you know about the case.)

What have you done about this situation so far?

What have thought about trying but haven't done yet? How might that be helpful?

GOAL FORMULATION
What does _____ (pressuring person or mandating agent) think you need to do differently? (Use these questions when the client starts out negative and seems to be unmotivated.)

Suppose you were to decide to do that, what would be different between you and _____ (pressuring person or agent)? (Continue with: ... different between you and _____ [significant others])

Is that something you could do?

What at a minimum would you say that you have to do differently?

When was the last time you did that? Suppose you were to decide to do it again, what would be the first small step you would take?

Miracle Question (Once asked, focus on *what will be different* when the miracle happens.)

Regarding client: What will you notice that's different? (What will be the first thing that you notice? What else?)

(continued)

Regarding significant others Who else will notice when the miracle happens?

What will s/he notice that is different about you? What else?

When s/he notices that, what will s/he do differently? What else?

When s/he does that, what will be different for you?

MOVING TOWARD A SOLUTION (Use when the client can answer the miracle question.)

Suppose you were to pretend that the miracle happened, what would be the first small thing you would do?

How might that be helpful?

Or: What's it going to take for a part of the miracle to happen?

Is that something which could happen? If so, what makes you think so?

ENDING
1. If the client is concrete and detailed in answer to the miracle question, give compliments and suggest: "In the next week, pick one day and pretend that the miracle has happened and look for what difference it makes."

2. If the client is *not* concrete and detailed in answer to the miracle question, give compliments and suggest: "Think about what's happening in your life that tells you that this problem can be solved. And I'll do some thinking too."

(If a second session is a possibility, you can ask the client to meet with you again to continue working on the problem.)

USEFUL QUESTIONS FOR USE WITH
INVOLUNTARY CLIENTS

1. Whose idea was it that you need to come here?
   What is your understanding of why you are here?

2. What makes _____ (pressuring person or mandating agent) think that you need to come here?
   What does _____ think you need to do differently?
   What does _____ think is the reason you have this problem?

3. What would _____ say that, at a minimum, you have to do differently?
   What do you have to do to convince _____ that you don't need to come here?

4. When was the last time that you did this (i.e. whatever the client said _____ said needs to be different)?
   What was different in your life then?
   How did you manage to do that?
   What do you think _____ (significant other) would say s/he noticed different about you then?

5. Suppose you were to decide to do that again, what would be the first step you would have to take to make it happen?
   How confident are you that you could do that again?
   What would it take to raise your confidence a bit?
   What would _____ (significant other) say the chances are that you will do this again?

6. Suppose you were to decide to do this, what would be different between you and _____ (significant other)?
   What would be different between you and _____ (pressuring person or mandating agent)?

7. Suppose you were to decide to do it, what other differences would it make in your life?
   What would be going on in your life that is not going on now?

8. How will you know when you have done enough?
   Who will be the first to notice when you make those changes?
   When _____ notices the changes, what will s/he do differently from what s/he does now? And, when s/he does that, how will that be for you?

ROLE CLARIFICATION

(There may be times when you would not start this way but be prepared to state your name and what you do in this setting.)

Say: I glad you came here today. I think you are in the right place. What kind of help do you need first?

Go slowly; accept and affirm client's perceptions.

CURRENT COPING EFFORTS (Assume competency.)

Find and compliment strengths, say: I'm glad you called, or I'm glad you made it here. I wonder how you did that.

What else are you doing to take care of yourself in this situation? (Get details: what, when, where, who, and how)

What else has been helpful to you?

Could it be worse than it is? How come it is not worse? (Notice and compliment strengths.)

Who (and what) do you think would be most helpful to you at this time?

What about them (and that) would be so helpful to you?

SCALING COPING PROGRESS

Suppose 10 means equals coping as well as you could possibly imagine, and 0 means not coping at all, where would you say you are at right now? _____

(If the number is 2 or above, be amazed/compliment and ask how s/he got all the way up to that number. If it is 1, ask about the first small coping steps. If it is 0 or below, ask what s/he is doing to prevent it from sliding further. Get details of coping thoughts and behaviors.)

(continued)

GOAL FORMULATION: CO-CONSTRUCTING THE NEXT STEP

Suppose things moved up one number on the scale, what would be different that would tell you that you were coping just that much better?" (Ask for small signs of improvement.)

What would _____ (significant other) notice different about you that would tell her or him that you were coping better? What else?

What would it take for that to happen?

Suppose things moved up 2 or 3 numbers on the same scale, what would be different that would tell you that you were coping that much better? What else? What would it take to make those things happen? What else? (Or, if the client is becoming more hopeful, ask the miracle question around "coping as well as anyone could imagine, considering what you have been through.")

What is the single most important thing for you to remember to continue coping with this situation?

ENDING

Summarize what the client is doing that is useful for her or himself. Be sure to point out small details using the clients own words. Compliment the client for his or her strengths and successes. Suggest that the client continue to do what works and pay attention to what else s/he may be doing that is useful for coping.

- How did you manage to get out of bed this morning?

    - Was it difficult for you?

    - What else was helpful so that you could do it?

- How long has it been since you last ate?

    - How has that been helpful to you?

    - How do you get yourself to eat?

- When is the last time that you got some sleep?

    - Has it made a difference?

    - With all you've been through, how do you manage to get to sleep?

- What has been helpful that got you through so far?

- What do you think we can do that would be most helpful?

- Have you been in this situation before?

    - What did you do to get through it then?

    - What was the most helpful to you?

    - Who helped you the most last time?

    - How did you know that _____ would be helpful?

    - What did you do to get _____ to help you?

    - What did _____ do that was so helpful to you? What else?

    - What would it take for _____ to help you again? What else?

    - When you get that help again, what difference will it make for you this time?

Appendix C
End-of Session Feedback
for Selected Clients on the Videotape

Second Session Feedback for Melissa

View Clips 6 and 7 on the videotape and formulate your own end-of-session feedback before comparing it to Kristin's.

Compliments

Kristin: Well, Melissa, so many things, positive things have happened to you and you've experienced so many positive things since the last time we've talked.

Melissa: Mm-hmm.

K   Sounds like the brainstorming we did the last time we talked as really been helpful for you.

M   Mm-hmm.

K   And I wanna compliment you on how you are continuing to balancing these things in your life.

M   Well, thanks.

K   How even just doing one little thing in the mornings or spending an afternoon with your children or a morning at school with them has been helpful for you and you've taken the motivation to do that.

M   Ya, ya, it's nice to especially do things outside of the house like going camping and going to their school. That helps a lot cuz it just gets me out of the mind set of, "Oh, look at all these chores." You know? House work is not my most favorite thing to do. It just, you know.

Bridge

K   And you're dealing with that fact in your life right now by considering the importance it has in your life right now.

M   Mm-hmm.

Task

K   Well, you know, you've made so much progress since last time we talked and I would just encourage you to keep doing what you're doing that you find helpful.

M   Oh thanks.

K   And keep looking forward to the summer when you can have some time off to concentrate on things that are important to you.

M   Yup.

K   But I just wanna thank you for coming in again today and if you'd like we can set up another appointment to talk.

M   Okay.

K   Okay? Thanks Melissa.

M   Yup, you too.

End-of-Session Feedback for Tim

View Clips 8 through 12 and formulate your own end-of-session feedback before comparing it to Peter's.

Compliments

Peter: Okay. So let me give you some of my impressions based on what we talked about so far. First off, I have to say how impressed I am that for six or seven months you basically have been taking care of those boys.

Tim: Ya.

P   You have some help from your sister, but you have basically, been doing this by yourself.

T   Yup, absolutely.

P   Through your sheer will and determination. And I wanna shake your hands on that, shake your hand on that. I think that that's a big accomplishment. That's a big accomplishment. It's also very clear to me that you care about your boys.

T   Absolutely. Ya, there's no doubt there.

P   And that bottom line in this is that you want to be with your boys and that you want them to have a home with their father and not be bounced around from place to place.

T   Ya, I don't want that.

P   Okay, okay. And I also wanted to say that I'm very impressed that as angry and frustrated as you are with what happened last week in court -

T   Ya.

P   And how that came out. I'm very impressed that in spite of that, you're able to look at your situation and think about and talk about what changes, even small changes, could be made that both impress the court and at the same time make the kind of home you wanna have for your boys.

T   Ya.

P   So you were talking about things like you'd like to spend more time with the boys.

T   Uh-huh.

P   Maybe go to Connor's school. Um, you were talking about not yelling as much. I forgot, what were you saying to do instead of yelling? What you'd like to see happen instead?

T   You know, do more things with them. Take them to the park. You know, read to them maybe. I don't know. Something like that.

P   That's very impressive to me. And a lot of people would be so angry with this situation that they couldn't think about those things, but you're thinking.

T   Oh, I'm thinking about, ya about my boys.

Bridge

P   Okay. And I agree with you. I think that following through on the expectations of the court is gonna make the biggest impression on the court.

T   Okay, okay.

Task

P   Um, that thinking on your part makes a lot of sense to me. Um, and I know that you're very interested in getting your boys back as soon as is possible. So the next one of the, the next pieces for us is to start work on this parent-agency agreement where we put down the things that you're going to do.

T   Oh, okay, okay.

P   Like, um, follow through on the alcohol assessment and the parenting classes and so forth. And um, then we both sign that.

T   Okay.

P   So I'm gonna get started based on the information that you gave me and draw up a preliminary parent-agency agreement.

T   Okay.

p   And then um, in about a week or ten days we'll sit down and we'll talk that through and see if that's still the way you see it.

T   Ya, that'd be great. Finally.

P   And we can talk about any adjustments in it that you wanna have made in it.

T   Okay.

P   Okay? I also heard that you're concerned about your job situation and that you have uh, some financial rent concerns right now.

T   Ya.

P   Um, and that even down the line you wanna be talking about day care, to get some, assuming the boys come back, that you'll have --

T   Oh, they'll come back.

P   -- day care, okay? And um, I think as we talk along about the parent-agency agreement, we can also talk about those things and how those things can happen, too. Okay? Um, so I think the next step is for me to get some information about when the parenting classes are, when and where about the alcohol assessment and get that scheduled. And of course, next step is to set up a visit.

T   Ya, about time.

P   Between you and your children.

T   Ya, absolutely.

P   So what I will do is when I get to the office I will call the foster parents.

T   Okay.

P   And I'll find out about their schedule. Um, are there any times which you couldn't meet the children?

T   Any day. I can meet with them any day. I can adjust my schedule no problem. That's my priority, ya.

P   Alright. So I will um, make that call and I will get back to you later today or tomorrow about that.

T   Uh, you know, like I don't have a phone. How are you gonna?

P   Ah, that's right. That's right. I will um, I can leave you my card.

T   Okay.

P   Which has my phone number on it.

T   Alright. That'd be good.

P   And um, you can give a call. If I'm not in my office you can, it's got a voice mail.

T   Okay.

P   You can ask to ring the secretary and I will leave the information with the secretary.

T   Oh, okay. Good, so I call later today or --

P   Ya, call between 4:30 and 5:00 today. I'll try to have it there.

T   Okay. Try to do that, ya.

P   Otherwise I'll have a message there about what happened and what to do next.

T   Okay. That would be great. Ya.

P   Okay? Um, is there anything else that we should talk about?

T   No, that's a lot right now. You know, it's a lot of information. So.

P   You have any questions?

T   Uh, not yet. You know, I'm sure I will as we go, definitely have questions.

P   Alright. Well, thanks again for meeting with me.

T   Thanks.

P   And um, I'll wait for your phone call.

T   Okay.

End-of-Session Feedback for Alex and Nancy (Mother)

View Clips 13 and 14 and formulate your own end-of-session feedback before comparing it to Insoo's.

Compliments

Insoo: Well, uh, Peter and I had some conversation and I just want to summarize what we talked about, the two of us talked about. Well, uh, we both are just absolutely, very impressed by both of you. And I will tell you why.

Nancy: Okay.

I   Wanna hear this? Well, obviously you both are very strong people, strong willed people, very opinionated, very definite ideas. And in spite of that there is such a loving, uh, willingness to listen to each other. You're open to hearing what the other person has to say. Uh, such respect for each other. Ya, I mean, and we have to tell you what a wonderful job you've done.

N   Oh thank you.

I   With Alex. I mean, you know, I mean, it's not been easy for you, obviously. Being a single mom is a full time job, a very stressful job. And raising you know, as you were saying, running here and there and you know. I mean, it has not been easy, but you really have done a very, I mean, Alex is such a nice young man. And uh, it's just very touching to hear him say that he would like to see Mom happy and calm.

N   That took my by surprise.

I   Yes. And how that affects him.

N   Mm-hmm.

I   When he sees you happy and calm he says he's also happier. So obviously you're very, very important to him. You know, I mean, I have to tell you that not only he's bright and smart, but he has such a nice way, I mean, he's so articulate. You know, most 15 year olds, sort of all we get out of them is a grunt here or there.

N   (laugh)

I   He's able to explain things and he has a definite point of view and he's willing to hang in there. He's patient, persistent. He has some definite ideas. I just have to really admire that. So I think that you both have this idea that, in spite of the fact that we disagree, that you are willing to talk to each other, continue to talk, continue to communicate. And then something might happen. It might.

N   It might.

I   It might. Right? And somehow it may. And also you both are saying when you are willing to listen to each other's ideas and then maybe, maybe you may come more toward the middle.

N   Right.

Bridge

I   Okay. And you're also saying that when you, instead of going in your bedroom and shutting your door, perhaps you're telling the children what kind of state of mind you are in. And perhaps you explaining to them and asking them might work better.

N   Right, right. I realize that, ya.

Task

I   Ya, so you have some clear ideas about what to do. And uh, I was just absolutely amazed. The fact that you had days like last Saturday is a very good, very good sign, very good indicators that you could have more days like last Saturday. Okay, so I would suggest, all I can suggest to you is just keep thinking about those things. Keep being open. And as you continue to do what you are doing, pay attention to what you are doing, what the other person is doing, what each of you are doing that gives you the idea that we are moving closer to six.

N   Okay. Sounds good.

I   Okay? Great. Well, thank you very much. Thank you for coming. And you, too. He has a beautiful smile.

N   Mm-hmm. (laugh)

I   Doesn't he, though? Beautiful smile. Oh, that could be a lady killer.

N   Oh, oh, we don't need to go there. (laugh)

I   Don't wanna do that, huh?

N   No, let's not go there.

I   Great. Okay. We're done.

End-of-Session Feedback for Karen

View Clips 18 through 21 and formulate your own end-of-session feedback before comparing it to Insoo's.

Compliments

Insoo: Uh, Karen, uh, I took some time to think about what we've been talking about and let me give you some of my thoughts about listening to you, lots of things I've been sort of you know, trying to make sense out of all this. First of all, it seems to me you've been very confused and not knowing, uncertainty. Do I go this way? Do I go that way? You're being angry. You're being disappointed. You're being embarrassed All this seems perfectly normal given the circumstances. And uh, however, in the midst of all this being a very confusing time for you, you found some ways to help yourself such as going to the movies, and crying about it, you hugging your children even though children were thinking about, "My gosh, what's going on," right?

Karen: Ya.

I   But you found some ways that are helpful for you. So I mean, you know, in the midst of all this, that's quite amazing, really, when you think about it. And that also tells me that you are a woman of a great deal of strength and seems --

K   I don't feel strong right now.

Bridge

I   I'm sure you don't. I'm sure you don't feel that way, but it just from, as an outsider looking in, that you have a definite idea that things have to change in the marriage. That Bob has to change, some things have to change. That's becoming very clear to you. And I absolutely agree with that. That's a very good idea. Um, there, you, I mean, it just seems like that's very, very clear and a very good idea. You also have a very clear idea about you need to talk to your mother. Your mother is your support person and you know how to use who is supportive of you.

Task

And it's also becoming much clearer to you that all you want to make a decision for now is just being away from everybody for a week and you're not going to make any decision before that, which is a very smart move. So I really support that. You know yourself very well in the midst of all this confusing time. And you know exactly what to do and I think it's a very good idea to not make any decision for a week instead of trying to put a lot of pressure on yourself. And perhaps this not knowing what to do, "Do I go this way or do I go this way? Do I do this or do I do that?" Perhaps that's a good thing for now because it prevents you from making a decision when you're not ready yet. And so it allows you to sit on it for awhile and I think it'll be a very good idea. So that, you know, something is telling you that you're not quite ready yet to make this big decision, so perhaps for awhile longer, you may need to make some more decisions. And until you get to this point, you don't know what the next point will be.

K   My mom always says, "Baby steps, baby steps."

I   Ya, baby steps, that's right. Sounds like your mom is a very wise woman.

K   She is.

I   Ya. So. Wow. Again, I'm very impressed with you that this kind of an event would have absolutely devastated most women, but here you are, you're still able to hang in there. Not only that, but you're able to think about your children's welfare, and you're also thinking about, "What do I need? What needs to change in my life?" And again, those are big decisions you need to make, ya. It is probably a good idea not to make this kind of big decision right now. Okay?

K   Okay.

I   Alright. Good luck.

K   Thank you.

I   Ya, okay.